Praise for 'Healthy Habits', a #1 Amazon Best Seller:

"Kate led me on a journey of self-rediscovery – who I am, what I value most, what and who to let go. She encouraged me to dream big and take the steps to achieve my goals. I learned how to overcome my self-criticism, prioritise self-care, regain my confidence and find a work-life-energy balance. I am incredibly grateful for Kate's wisdom, support and guidance. I am truly happy and in love with my life. Thank you Kate"

-       Kristy

"Where some may imagine that they can't possibly have the courage and confidence to make positive life changing decisions by themselves, you provide exactly the direction and support so that although guidance is there, ultimately the decision, direction and change is made by the participant. Like myself, only then can your participants take those positive changes and make them permanent – when they've ultimately been the decision maker. Now that is a sign of a magnificent coach."

-       Alice Nicholls (The Whole Daily)

"I love this book, thank you Kate for guiding me through achievable strategies to improve my health and happiness.

Beautifully written and easy to follow.

I highly recommend this book."

-       Kim McPherson (The Well Nurse)

"A straight forward, matter of fact, easy reading lifestyle book with many clever insights and revelations for today's busy woman who tries to have it all. Makes you realise what is really important in the whole scheme of things."

-      Chris

"This world was not always easy to travel through but I maintain that it is the first time in my 20 years that I felt any kind of self-awareness, and I thank Kate for that. It was the first time I'd ever bothered to identify my values, my beliefs and more about who I am. In fact, I'm planning on starting it all over again, but for the moment, my anchor is down and I'm processing what I have already learnt about myself. Thank you Kate for helping me to figure out who I am."

-      Peta Kelly

"Well written and inspiring, something for every busy woman - and man. Commit to the purchase, read it, choose a few actions from the many suggestions, and voila, enjoy a healthier, happier you!"

-      Kylie Bevan

"I have been so blessed to work with Kate this year. She is a true inspiration to those wanting to transform their life and she does it in such a gentle, manageable way. Kate is gorgeous, healthy and funny and really walks her talk!"

-      Nicole Beardsley (The Happy Parent Project)

HEALTHY HABITS

Healthy Habits

The Busy Woman's Guide to Boosting Productivity, Health and Happiness

Kate Toholka

Foreword by Lisa Messenger

Editor in Chief, Renegade Collective

A NUMBER 1 AMAZON BEST SELLER

DISCLAIMER

The people and events described and depicted in this book are for educational purposes only. While every attempt has been made to verify that the information provided in this book is correct and up to date, the author assumes no responsibility for any error, inaccuracy or omission.

If advice concerning legal or related matters is needed, the services of a qualified profession should be sought. This book is not intended for use as a source of professional medical advice. You are expected to be aware of any law that governs any financial and business transactions or other business practices in your State or Region.

The success examples in this book are not intended to represent or guarantee that everyone or anyone will achieve their desired results. Every individual's success is determined by a number of varying factors, which include her or her desire, dedication, effort and motivation. The tools, stories and information are provided as examples only, not as sources of professional medical advice. You understand that every change in lifestyle has inherent risk factors on your health. Please seek a consulting doctor before you embark on a lifestyle transformation.

National Library of Australia

Cataloguing in Publication Entry:

Kate Toholka 1987

Healthy Habits: The Busy Woman's Guide to Boosting Productivity, Health and Happiness

Stress management for women.

Women--Health and hygiene.

Happiness.

Health behavior.

Holistic medicine.

ISBN-10: 0992466601

ISBN-13: 978-0-9924666-0-2

158.72

QUANTITY PRINT ON DEMAND ORDERS AVAILABLE

By International Best Selling Author Kate Toholka, Healthy Habits is available at special quantity discounts for bulk purchases to be included for marketing, promotions, fundraisers and or educational purposes.

Free chapters are also available to promote to your clients or give away as a gift with the option to purchase the full Print or Digital copy of the book.

Contact kate@summersaltlife.com.au to discuss how we can accommodate your needs.

Or visit our website at

http://www.summersaltlife.com.au

Self-Published

PO Box 302, Torquay Vic 3228.

Dedication

To my two loves, Timmy and Hershey. Thank you for making my life so awesome.

Contents

Join the Healthy Habit Community today!

This book is only the beginning of your journey towards a rich, rewarding life. There's a whole lot more fun and games at www.summersaltlife.com.au.

To really ingrain our healthy habits, we need to be surrounded by a supportive community. Connection with others is paramount to all success in any areas of our lives. I know that without a doubt, I would not have been able to instil my own healthiest habits without a posse of empowering, positive, uplifting women to keep me accountable and push me to where I wouldn't dare go alone. I want you to have this empowering posse too.

I've put together more resources, handy hints and a bubble of empowering love just for you. Join me at **www.summersaltlife.com.au** and learn how you can:

- **Join our inspiring online community.**

Connect with other women who are driven to become the best versions of themselves. Share the love. Support each other. Make new friends.

- **Download a growing body of free resources.**

I am continually updating and creating great resources to help you create your healthiest and happiest life. Stay informed and stay inspired with the free blog.

• **Download your free Healthy Habit resources and watch the video.**

Go to www.summersaltlife.com.au/healthyhabits and enter your details to receive printable copies of all the resources as mentioned in this book. Print them. Answer them. Use them.

• **Access exclusive programs, interviews, videos, webinars, and articles**

Once this book is in your hands, I can't update it. But I can update the content on my site. So pop over there to stay up to date with all the new lessons and tools I develop.

• **Connect with us on social media**.

I love social media. I love how it connects us in so many ways. And I'd love to connect with you. My personal favourite is Instagram (@summersaltlife) but you can also find me on: Facebook (facebook.com/summersaltlife), Pinterest (pinterest.com/summersaltlife) and Twitter (@summersaltlife).

Visit **summersaltlife.com.au** to really take this book to the next level.

FOREWORD

By Lisa Messenger

CEO of The Messenger Group and Editor-in-Chief of Renegade Collective.

As the CEO of the Messenger Group and Editor-in-Chief of Renegade Collective magazine, I know a thing or two about busyness. Pressing deadlines and rushing to meetings are the daily norm in my hectic world.

Being an entrepreneur can be quite stressful. I've had my fair share of ups and downs in the last 12 years since I began my first business. I've learnt that I need to be able to manage my stress as best as I can. We can't avoid stress in the workplace – it's a given! Instead we need to manage our responses as best as we can. And that can be as simple as setting boundaries. We can't just go hard every single day, breaking down bodies and minds in the process. We need to stop and smell the roses. Set limits. Take charge of our wellness. Get our productivity hat back on.

Managing our stress takes more than just deep breathing exercises. It takes a change in our eating habits, even our drinking habits. This is something that Kate advocates wisely and simply. The simple concept of eating nourishing real food and eating it mindfully can really reduce our stress levels.

On the other hand, it takes a change of mindset. To go from "I can't cope with this" to "I am energised and inspired to do this". To work with our natural stress responses, instead of making the situation worse.

I have long been a staunch advocate for following your passions and finding your purpose in life. For me, it involved a lot of praying to the universe and letting go of my attachment to outcomes. But in the face of busyness, it's so easy to disconnect with our true purpose. Kate clearly explains how this conscious reconnection can be the driving force behind a happier, healthier life. By knowing, by truly believing in your purpose every single day, can help you create the life you want.

There's a difference between busyness and productiveness. One that I believe has its base in our wellbeing. Knowing your purpose may be the first step, but taking charge of your whole wellbeing is going to do wonders for your productivity. Plus, we may find that being more productive makes us less busy. Wouldn't that be a miracle?

Whether you are an entrepreneur, inspiring entrepreneur or happily working for your boss, take heed of your health. Life becomes rich with meaningful experiences when we are well enough to enjoy them.

Be well, live in the moment.

Lisa x

Lisa Messenger

Editor-in-Chief,

Renegade Collective

www.renegadecollective.com

www.facebook.com/collectivehub

www.twitter.com/lisamessenger

Introduction

"Never get so busy making a living

that you forget to make a life." – Anon.

Busy women don't really like it when they're told to relax more. We can't think of anything worse than someone telling us to "chill out, take some time off!" when we're experiencing a full blown stress attack. No, busy women don't want to do that. We want to get more done in less time and with less stress. We want to cultivate productive, happy, and healthy habits.

We have so many things going on at once that it gets overwhelming and exhausting at times. We're expected to hold the title of mum-career woman-daughter-sister- friend-house keeper-wife-lover-carer-superwoman with ease and beauty. We're expected to do so much in so little time. It's no wonder we're burnt out!

Stress is the biggest culprit for busy women. It underlies all our negative habits. Hence, this book will focus on how you can best manage your stress through a range of holistic strategies. Reducing stress is essential to creating sustainable, healthy habits.

The Glorification of Busyness

Isn't it funny how we say, "Oh, I've been so busy!" like it's a badge of honour? It's like we get immediate social standing when we highlight that we are too busy to do anything like, well, *nothing*.

Western culture is all about doing everything at once. We have gadgets that make our business run ten times faster. We've become a nation of multi-tasking extraordinaire queens. We create technologies that do things for us. And we pay our hard earned dollars for people to do our dreaded menial jobs. The whole concept of taking it slow and easy is for the alternative, hippy, bush-loving environmentalist. Not the savvy, sophisticated, hard-working woman.

If I started a revolution, it would be a revolution against 'busyness.' We are not meant to be running around with deadlines and people pulling us left, right and centre. The fast-paced lifestyle has only really taken off in the last 50 or so years.

Think back to our ancestors, thousands of years ago, or even a hundred years ago. Their pace of lifestyle was slow, very slow. They didn't need to run around town or call fifty people a day. Clearly they didn't have the technology back then, but technology has enabled us to fast forward our lifestyle at a phenomenal speed. We have the potential to do so much more in much less time! Therefore we feel like we should be doing so much more in much less time. Our bodies simply have not evolved (yet!) to withstand the constant stressors we place on ourselves.

A complete change of lifestyle from one that's busy to one that's slow can be a reality for those who actively seek it. However, I'm well aware that it's not a reality for most of us. Nor is it a wanted reality for many. That's why I've written this book. It's your handbook to coping with your busyness as best as you can, so that you can get more done without running yourself into the ground.

The Problem with Chronic Stress

In the next chapter, I talk about the concept of stressing better, not less. Stress is an inevitable part of being human. It's our survival mechanism and in-built alarm to prepare our bodies to save ourselves in the face of threats. However, stress becomes the threat itself when it becomes prolonged.

I'm sure you've heard of all the various ailments and diseases you should expect if you experience chronic stress. Heart disease, stroke, diabetes, arthritis, Alzheimer's, anxiety, depression are all candidates. You could even argue that all diseases have an element of chronic stress to them. There is no doubt that having constant and prolonged stress is going to be harmful for our health.

This is not a medical book so I'm not going to go into detail about how stress works and impacts us on a cellular, physiological level. You can find that information with a simple Google search. I will talk in detail about the body's natural stress mechanism in Chapter 1 but that's about the deepest I will go into the scientific literature. Instead of boring you with the science mumbo jumbo of how chronic stress is going to kill you (it will, just saying!), I'm going to talk about the greater, hidden danger of chronic stress. This is the concept of wasting your time and killing your dreams.

Bad Habits and Stress Will Kill Your Dreams

Chronic stress can eat away at your precious time. It can cause you to spend more time feeling lethargic, exhausted, anxious, and outright sad. It saps away our energy leaving us to fight for the good times. It generally makes our lives an unpleasant experience. It in turn creates bad habits. Bad habits are notorious for wasting time (procrastination anyone?). Combined, it's a recipe for disaster when trying to achieve our dreams and goals.

Stress has the ability to take away our hope. We get so caught up in the situation of getting more done, or doing things to a certain standard, that we lose sight of the bigger picture. We lose sight of what is really important to us and how we want to really spend our precious time.

It cripples us into analysis paralysis, and can literally hold us back from doing the things we really want to do. Chapter 2 explores this in detail, but for now I want you to take a moment to think back to a time you didn't do something you would have liked to do because it was too stressful.

Have you ever had a dream or desire to do something so great and daring but it was too fearful and stressful to pursue?

Stress and fear go hand in hand. We react with stress when we're fearful. Together they're so powerful in holding us back! We can spend more of our precious time being more fearful and stressed than we do in pursuing all the things we really want to do.

I've written this book with the clear aim of helping you live your life on your terms. Every bit of advice I give is all about getting you to truly become alive. Life is to be enjoyed, after all.

What to Expect

This book is all about giving you simple strategies in eight key areas of your life to help reduce the impact of stress through cultivating healthy habits. It's not your standard 'relaxation' or 'take a chill pill' kind of book. It includes relaxation strategies for sure, but that's just part of the picture. It's in fact a different approach to managing your stress.

It is holistic, meaning we look at all areas of your life. It is preventative, meaning we look at how to prevent chronic, ongoing stress. It is a mindset change, meaning we redefine our approach to stress and stressful situations. It is in fact, a re-approach to stress management. Effective stress management is the key to cultivating healthy habits and happiness.

Each chapter covers a particular area in detail. I've written this book with you in mind – the hard working, multi-tasking, health-conscious working woman. I know you don't have time to read a 500-page novel and I know you don't really care about the smaller print. You just want facts and an action plan. I'm not going to beat around the bush. I'll be getting straight to the point. I'm going to give you the low down of each area and the key things you really need to know. It will be direct, simple and relevant to you!

Checklists

I have provided you with a list of strategies you can begin implementing immediately at the end of each chapter. You don't have to do them all, but it's recommended that you try at least two from each list. Give each strategy a go at some point though – you're more likely to find something that works best for you. You can use the bonus resources found with the video to help you implement them into your daily routine.

Real Women, Real Stories

It's really helpful to know that we're not alone. Throughout the book, I share real life stories of hard working women who have managed their stress holistically using the strategies I have outlined in the book. They are all hard working, successful women who are living their passions in face of all their stressors. I have included them to inspire you and remind you that we are all here for you.

Bonus resources

I have created a web page that has all the extra resources (completely free!) to help you create your lasting healthy habits. The link to this page is summersaltlife.com.au/healthyhabits and the password to access this page is: healthyhabits. You will find a video plus a number of printable PDF documents, including worksheets, fact sheets and resource lists. This is the extra kick to get you into action.

Get Ready

It's time. It's time to no longer be the stressed out wonder woman. Let's turn you into a vivacious, healthy, glowing woman who gets more done instead!

Make a commitment with yourself to do what you need to do to make the changes you're looking for. You can read this book a hundred times over but until you actually implement what you learn, you will not get the benefit.

It's very helpful to make a conscious pledge to change. It helps you to set the intention you're after. We explore the concept of visualization more in Chapter 3, but the idea is to visualize exactly what, where and who you want to be. Take a moment to visualize exactly that. Then take this pledge:

I am willing to change my life for the better. I am prepared to do what I need to do so stress and bad habits no longer rule my life. I am a strong, fierce woman capable of limitless possibilities. I am ready to change the behaviours that are holding me back. I am ready to break through the limiting beliefs I hold. I am a strong, fierce, successful woman and I am not alone. I am one with my fellow women and together we are going to create a healthier, happier place!

Chapter 1: The Re-Approach

"Man should not try to avoid stress any more than

he would shun food, love, or exercise." – Dr Hans Selye

There are hundreds of books out there touting the best stress management techniques to get you stressing less. You can do a simple Google search and you will find an unlimited list of techniques at your disposal.

So why would I write another stress management book to add to the never-ending list? Because I believe those techniques are only parts of the picture. The whole picture is missing. I've tried every stress management technique under the sun, and I'm sure you have too. Some work, some don't. Some work sometimes, and don't at other times. Some are just plain unhealthy or only a short-term fix.

We need to approach stress management from a totally new angle. An approach that focuses on the bigger picture, which calls for big changes with small steps.

This approach incorporates eight key areas of your life that need to be considered. They are:

1. **Restart:** A process of reflecting on how you use your time and your attitude towards life to allow quick and effective changes to get your new momentum for life going.

2. **Refocus:** Focusing on what's really important to you by finding your purpose in life.

3. **Renourish:** Learning how food impacts your ability to manage stress and how to find your own unique diet.

4. **Reenergize:** Exploring how movement and stillness in harmonic balance is vital to having a healthy body, mind and life.

5. **Rethink:** Creating a different relationship with your thoughts so that the most troubling thoughts no longer derail your choices.

6. **Reaccept:** Preventing emotional outbursts by learning to have a healthier relationship with your feelings instead of bottling them.

7. **Reconnect:** Acknowledging the importance of relationships with others and yourself in preventing and managing your stress response.

8. **Replenish:** Appreciate the value of interaction with nature and the environment in healing your body from stress.

Each area is equally important. The Re-Approach is a holistic approach. We need to look at the whole picture to make the most effective changes that last. Before we get into the nitty-gritty of each area, it's important to recognize that a key part of the Re-Approach is to look at stress itself in a whole new light.

Stress Free isn't the Answer, Stress Better Is

Yes, you read that right. The aim is to stress better, not to be stress-free. We are forever inundated with the message that we need to stop stressing altogether to live longer, happier, healthier lives. We are led to believe that any type of stress can cause us harm. The thing is though, stress is natural. You simply cannot eliminate stress from your life for good. Managing your stress better will essentially result in you having less stress but to strive for a completely stress-free existence is going to set you up for failure.

I'm sure you've heard of the Fight or Flight Response. It's our body's acute physiological response in the face of danger. It is automatic, primitive, and inborn. It enables us to run, fight or even freeze from a perceived attack, harm or any threat to our survival.

Our bodies release a hefty dose of chemicals such as adrenaline and cortisol once this response is activated. Our pupils dilate, pulse quickens, and our breathing becomes quick and haggard. Our perception of pain diminishes and our immune system mobilizes with increased activation. Our senses are on high alert. We see more, hear more, practically perceive more from our environment as we 'look for our enemy.' Our body essentially prepares itself physiologically and mentally to face the threat.

In this state, we literally perceive everything as a possible threat. Everything bypasses our rational mind, leading us to distort 'safe' events into exaggerated, catastrophic nightmares. We literally see everything through a filter of fear – fear becomes the lens through which we see our world.

So imagine if you are constantly and consistently stressed. You won't be able to cultivate a positive attitude. You won't be able to rationalize or make effective decisions. Your heart won't be open. You would only have the capability to survive. Which, granted, is ok but think about this – you won't be able to thrive. Do you really want to get by every single day doing the bare minimum you need to do to just survive, or would you rather thrive with the limitless possibilities you really have? When we live from crisis to crisis, we are destined to burn out. It's inevitable, regardless of how invincible you think you are. It will manifest into physical and/or emotional symptoms.

Know Your Signs

Stress doesn't always show up as the 'feeling' of being stressed. Therefore we need to get better at knowing our own stress cues. They are generally divided into two types: physical and psychological.

Physical symptoms are the easiest to spot, but the hardest to link to stress. Think about getting a headache for example. You may associate it with not drinking enough water and that it has nothing to do with being stressed. Other physical symptoms may include muscle tension, stomach complaints, deep sighing or shallow breathing. You may experience stress-induced conditions such as eye twitching or even tooth grinding. Maybe you find yourself increasingly restless and have started to fidget excessively. These are all possible physical manifestations of too many stress hormones. Personally, I get extreme muscle tension in my upper back and shoulders when I'm stressed. I know that I must do something to relax once I feel this – it's the very first warning sign that I'm 'under attack.'

Some women may notice that they tend to manifest more psychological symptoms rather than physical symptoms. Anxiety, short temper, irritability, poor concentration, depression and feeling scared for no apparent reason are excellent, and very common, examples.

It's really important to know how stress manifests in your body. It's even more important to know the very first cue. Once you're aware of this cue, the quicker you're able to recognize what is happening and to reverse the stress response as quickly as possible. Remember, the aim isn't to stress less in terms of how often you actually stress (though that obviously can be helpful – we will discuss that in a second) but it's to keep it short and acute, just the way it's meant to be.

Chronic Stress is the Killer, Not Stress Itself

We know we experience lots of stressors. Some that we can change, others that are out of our reach. However, the one thing we always can change is how we respond to the situation.

When our bodies go into Fight or Flight mode, our bodies are preparing for battle. Your blood flow has increased to get more oxygen to your muscles, your pupils have dilated to enable you to take more of your surroundings in. Your digestion and fertility system shut down so that vital systems (i.e. your neurological and cardiovascular systems) get all the attention they need to get you out of the dangerous situation as quickly as possible.

We've been conditioned to believe that this is causing all our biggest health concerns. Truthfully, it is when it's chronic and ongoing. But it's a natural, healthy response when it is used as it should be – a short burst of energy to get you out of your pickle as quick as possible.

Therefore, the aim is to use our stress response effectively, as it should be used. When we consciously acknowledge this fact, we are more inclined to go with our natural systems and respond quickly and effectively to the threat at hand.

There is a brilliant TED talk by health psychologist Kelly McConigal who talks about the research implicating the impact of believing stress is bad for you. The research produced some startling figures: over 182,000 Americans died prematurely over a period of 8 years, not from stress, but believing stress is bad for you. That works out to be over 20,000 people a year, which would make it the 15th largest cause of death in the US, killing more people than skin cancer, AIDS and homicide. Watch Kelly's talk to find out how the research uncovered this finding.

I don't want you to stop stressing altogether. It's not possible. I want you to go with your natural mechanisms and use stress just as it should be used – an acute burst of energy to help you beat your perceived threat.

The Biggest Threat You'll Ever Face

Let's go back to the definition of the Fight or Flight Response.

It's the body's natural coping mechanism to perceived danger.

The keyword here is 'perceived.' Back in the day, the perceived dangers were the very real dangers of the natural environment. Think bloodthirsty carnivores, turbulent weather, or travelling untouched plains with no idea what's coming around the corner.

Luckily we don't face those types of fears anymore. Well, not on a regular basis anyway. Instead we have a whole different range of perceived fears lurking at every corner. Deadlines, traffic jams, loud kids, bills, mortgages, horrible bosses, social agendas, political woes and the list goes on. The list of stressors for hard working women like yourself would be of mammoth proportions.

Women in particular, are expected to be the queens of multi-tasking. We're expected to find a loving partner, start a family, forge a career, have a clique of best friends and look after our own parents when needed. We're also faced with social prejudice, gender inequality and the killer of all, our own superwomen expectations.

In fact, our own expectations are the roots of most, if not all, our perceived fears. We are in fact, our own biggest threat. Busy women place immense pressures on themselves to be better, fitter, stronger, healthier, and more successful than other busy women. It creates a nasty environment that we all hate. But we are the ones that create it! Learning how to let go of our own fears will go a long way in creating your healthy habits.

Real Women, Real Stories

Erin Smallbon, of ES Wellness

For a long time, stress seemed to be a natural part of my life. I would be travelling along happy for a while and then suddenly things would build up, overwhelm would dawn on me and next thing I knew I was a full blown angry, hungry and emotional mess.

Times have changed thankfully and these days I use a many pronged approach when managing stress. I approach it holistically and I have developed many tools in my tool kit which I turn to on a daily basis to keep myself feeling the way I want to feel.

I keep stressful exercise to a minimum and prefer Pilates, yoga and walking as my exercise of choice. Nature is a balm for my soul and bush walking, sitting outside in the sun or a trip to the beach always manages to soothe me. I feel so at home at the beach. It re-energises me and never fails to transform my emotions.

Nutrition, which fuels and nourishes my body and does not stimulate it, is so important for me when managing stress. Caffeine, alcohol and sugar provide a stress on my body which I don't cope with well. I choose to try and minimise these foods and eat foods which keep me grounded, nourished and fulfilled.

The development of my spiritual practice is the cornerstone to allowing me to remain stress free. I now meditate and journal daily, which allows me to still my mind and access my creativity. I have done, and continue to do, the inner work to clear away the limiting beliefs which used to keep me in my glass box. I seek to follow my intuition when making decisions, to not over think things, to go with the flow more and I have realised that this life does not need to be about struggle. I have full control over my perception of my world and full control over the responses I have to my life.

Tough Love

You're a tough woman, I know that. So I'm going to be brutally honest with you here.

– **Don't expect the changes to be easy, or quick.** In fact, expect things to gradually get better. Each small change you make will add to the momentum. Momentum breeds momentum so we want to make it the good kind. Have faith that every little thing you are doing will pay off for you.

– **It's an all or nothing approach**. Don't just pick one area and focus solely on that. The aim is to do a little of each. Remember, small steps lead to big changes.

– **Balance is the key**. Balance is everything. Learn to accept the idea of balance in every aspect of your life and in every moment of your life. Nothing is ever completely great or completely heart breaking.

– **You are responsible for your health and life.** No one else is. Acknowledge this responsibility and treat it with the love it deserves. Laying blame on others for our woes is a recipe for disaster. Taking ownership for all our flaws, imperfections, tribulations and uniqueness is an important step to creating the life you're after.

– **All changes start with you**. I get it. It'd be nice if they'd change too, of if that never happened. But much like I just said above, you have to make the changes yourself. And this includes how you respond to things.

– **Don't be afraid to do what you need to do.** You might go through this book and start realizing that doing all the little things is working great, but you have a nagging feeling you need to do something big. It could be changing your career. Or taking time off work. Or going on a worldwide escape. Don't shy away from what you really believe you need to do. You can do it girl.

– **Start now.** Don't wait until you have a crippling illness or disability. Or when you have reached the end of your tether! Start making the changes right now. Chronic stress leads to a host of life-threatening illnesses, which take time to develop. You not only want to prevent these experiences, you want to ensure that you're living the life you want every single day. Don't wait for anything good or bad.

The Re-Approach is going to be by your side for the rest of your life. The struggle you feel right now with making these necessary changes won't last long, I assure you. The more you do them, the easier they become. They will become second nature in no time!

Chapter 2: Restart

"They always say time changes things,

but you actually have to change them yourself." - Andy Warhol

---

The problem many busy women face is running out of time. They get too swept up in the crazy momentum that things become increasingly overwhelming. When we get stuck in this momentum our stress levels rise and rise, reaching a boiling point.

This boiling point will manifest into a physical and/or mental breakdown of the body. We start to see our weight creep up around our stomachs, our hair gets thin and wispy and wrinkles start to form at a horrifying rate. Therefore it's really, really important for women to not reach this boiling point. You're most likely at this point now if you're reading this, so the key for you is to not reach that point again. You need to restart.

Restarting is all about wiping the slate clean and doing something super effective, super quick. It's about looking at two things: how you spend your time and your attitude towards life.

Time Use

You might have a clear idea of how you use your time. Maybe you have a diary where you record all your appointments, schedules, and things to do. I'm willing to bet though that even if you do have a pretty full diary, it wouldn't include everything you do every minute of the day.

• What do you do in between meetings?

• Do you spend time traveling, on the phone or browsing the internet?

• How much time at work do you actually spend working?

• How much time do you spend on shiny things, like the king procrastination tool, a.k.a the internet?

It's really important to have a good understanding of how you use your time exactly. Your main aim as a hardworking woman would be to get more done in less time with better stress. If you're wasting your time on low value activities (which we will discuss in more detail in Chapter 4), you're encouraging more stress.

Moreover, time is precious. As I said in the Introduction, our time is our most valuable asset. We all have the same amount of hours in our days as everyone else – even Beyoncé!

It's what we do with our time that is most important. We can never make up for lost time. We can only do what we can with the time we have left. Therefore it is so important to know exactly how you use your time.

Mindset

Mindset is defined as a "fixed mental attitude or disposition that predetermines a person's responses to and interpretations of situations" according to FreeDictionary. Mindset ultimately means your attitude. How you approach your life and the stressful situations that go with it are testament to how you cope.

Mindfulness is one very powerful tool in changing our mindset. It can be done very effectively in short amount of time. Therefore it is the best tool to restart your mindset.

The Art of Mindfulness

There's an old saying by Lao Tzu that covers how important mindset is in relation to stress:

"If you are depressed, you are living in the past. If you are anxious, living in the future. If you are at peace, you are living in the moment."

We become overwhelmed with stress when we focus too much on the future. We can be so blinded by deadlines, to-do lists and double-bookings that we can't see a glimmer of hope of ever getting anything done. Then we start to feel depressed and frustrated that we can't do everything we need to do. It's a vicious cycle.

Busy women need to learn how to change their mindset from the future to the present. We need to rewind and restart our minds to the here and now. Women who give their full attention to the task at hand, instead of worrying about how they're going to do everything on their to-do lists, are much more effective, relaxed and successful in their lives.

Meditation and mindfulness are huge buzz words in the health industry, and rightfully so because they do amazing things for the body and mind. Mindfulness is best explained as the concept of tuning all your senses into the present moment.

Consider where you are right now. What do you see? What can you smell? Take a moment to look around the room you are in right now. Take note of everything you see, hear, smell, feel and taste. That is what mindfulness is about. It's about letting go of our stories (which I will explain further in Chapter 6) and tuning into our immediate surroundings.

Meditation, which incorporates mindfulness, tends to refer to the practice that is entwined with Buddhism and Yoga, karma and reincarnation, gurus and ultimate truths, spirituality and New Age ideas. It basically comes from an ancient monastic tradition based on withdrawal from the world. Mindfulness is essentially entry-level meditation

In Chapter 5, I explain how meditation is extremely helpful. It's an excellent healthy habit to put into your routine. I understand that the idea of spending more than five minutes each day in utter stillness can be completely incomprehensible for a hard working woman. It can seem like a waste of time. I assure you it's not.

Meditation is a great stress management, self-development and spiritual awakening practice. Regardless of how pressed you feel for time, developing a mindfulness practice is essential to managing your stress levels and should be the bare minimum that you do. You just need to find creative ways to incorporate it into your daily routine.

Restart Now

When we're busy, and particularly when we're stressed, we don't realise exactly how we are using our time. We're definitely not using our time effectively if we're stressed out. The number one thing you need to do right now is schedule 30-60 minutes into your diary to focus on restarting.

Do it right now.

Open your diary, find a free hour and book it in. Treat it like an appointment with yourself. In fact, it's a very important appointment as this will prepare you to take your life to the next level. And the next-level includes more success, more happiness and better productivity. So do not under any circumstances change this VIP appointment! I promise you that you will not make the changes you need if you do not do this. You may as well put this book down and continue living a stressful life until you burn out into an unhappy, unhealthy mess.

Plan this appointment like you would any other appointment. Set yourself up in your office or someplace quiet where you will not be distracted. Take yourself to the nearby coffee shop or park if a change of scenery can help. If possible, turn your phone off or encourage people to not contact you during this time. If you have scheduled this time after working hours, let your family or partner know what you are doing. Arrange your partner or a babysitter to take the kids for the time. Another option would be to go to bed an hour earlier and do this before going to sleep.

Preparing for Your VIP Appointment

You will be spending a portion of time at your VIP appointment looking over your time use. To have a crystal clear picture of exactly how much of a hard worker you really are, keep a Time Diary for a few days. You can find a free copy to print on the resource page at summersaltlife.com.au/healthyhabits. The password to access this page is 'healthyhabits'.

The aim is to record every single thing you do for every minute of the day. Be 100% honest. Record absolutely everything – when you ate, travelled, spoke on the phone, had meetings, took a coffee break, procrastinated on Facebook, showered, everything!

The absolute first step is awareness and I guarantee you will be surprised at exactly how you spend your time. Take note of how you felt doing certain things. Were you inspired, happy and thriving? Or struggling, frustrated and bored? This extra insight is really helpful in identifying your time wasters.

Try to complete your time diary on your regular days, or even better, the days you consider more stressful. I recommend doing it for two weeks, however it's completely up to you how long you want to record your time use.

The second thing you need to do is finish this book. You can use the time in your VIP appointment to consolidate your thoughts from this book and develop a plan to implement everything you've learnt. This book will help you stress better and live successfully and healthy, but only when you implement the strategies.

Your VIP Appointment

The aim of this appointment with yourself is to focus on your time use and mindset. Begin your appointment by centering yourself through a short mindfulness strategy. Find a five minute body scan meditation online and listen to this (Fact: I mention my favourite on the video and yes, it's free). This will bring you to the present and allow you to wholeheartedly be there for your VIP appointment with yourself.

Look over your time diary and identify common themes. What things are you doing that could be classified as productive, time-wasting, necessary, stressful, or enjoyable? You might identify other themes but these are a great starting point.

The most important thing you need to do is to recognise the things you are doing that are causing you undue stress. If the concept of 'having no time' is your biggest stress, you need to identify the things you are doing that you consider being 'time wasters.'

How many minutes slip by when you're browsing Facebook or playing around on Instagram? Now, it's completely ok if you're doing that in a meaningful, productive, life-enriching sense. But if it's wiling away your time and completely pointless to you, it needs to go on your 'time wasters' list. Ask yourself – "Does doing this provide meaning to me?"

I strongly recommend you finish reading Chapter 2 at a minimum (if not, the whole book!) before your VIP appointment as this will make answering this question much easier for you.

The second half of your VIP appointment with yourself is to focus on your mindset. Go over your time use diary again and take note of your positive and negative experiences, as stated by the feelings you have recorded.

•   Do you find that you tend to be more negative than positive, or vice versa?

•   Are you more or less inspired most of the time?

Note down how often you're mindful (that is, in the present moment) and how often you're caught up in the momentum. Also note how prolonged your stress experiences are. This can be a really challenging task as it can be a real wake up call. Remember that awareness is the first step and without it, you won't be able to change what you need to change. Keep this in mind and remind yourself that it is a necessary step to creating your best life.

Once you've noticed all your patterns, it's time to change the patterns that need changing. Choose all the patterns that are bringing you down, tiring you out, wasting your precious time and vow to discard them for good. These bad habits are both how you spend your time and how you approach your life. They can be anything from procrastinating on Twitter to being negative about going to work. Start replacing those bad habits with good ones. It's up to you to figure out exactly what and how you will do that. This book will help you.

Aim to introduce a minimum of two strategies from this book into your daily routine immediately. You will find that many strategies don't require much effort. In fact, they are all small little changes that you can implement immediately without deviating too far from your original routine. They will quickly become a part of your new routine. Create a 'Re-Intention' action plan, listing all the strategies you are going to implement immediately. You should aim to implement one strategy from each area. Review this action plan frequently and continue to implement more strategies as you go along.

Finish your VIP appointment with another short meditation to again center yourself in the present moment. Retake the pledge from the Introduction and place your new re-intention plan somewhere visible where you will see it daily. You have done everything you need to do to kick start your new way of living. But it's only the kickstart. Feed this momentum by redoing your VIP appointment every few months and remember, you're in this for the rest of your life.

Real Women, Real Stories

Suzzi Hartery, of Nourished Hub

It all started when I was studying at university full time and working casually. I soon discovered I would have to work full time hours to move into a life I thought I wanted. I ended up taking university externally and working full-time in a skill-building company. I was working long hours because of underlying beliefs and needs.

I worked from 6am till often 11pm at night in the one job. I would have to get lifts to and from work as most time no transport was available or parking was more expensive then it was worth. My health started to decline and I turned into an ice cold bitch. I was skipping meals, not eating right and wasting my weekends with binge drinking. I began to lose sight of right and wrong.

I knew something was wrong when eventually I gained panic attacks listening to morning radio. My path had to change and it changed in a big way. I lost my job, the previous friends around me. But I gained so much more. I gained self-respect, self-belief and I gained love and confidence in my abilities.

What troubled me is that stress took a massive toll on me and I almost lost the love of my life and did career suicide (this is the first time I have ever said this out loud). I ran my life on other peoples beliefs, worrying about what others thought of me while trying to bring down others who I thought were better than me. I coped by first taking a hard good look at who I was,

what was going on around me and said goodbye. I started a journey which had been speaking to me for years. A journey of knowing no one's path is perfect, no one person is perfect and that what I had to offer in this world was uniqueness just like every single person in this life.

Stress can either take you down a huge spiral staircase or you can learn from it. Whenever I feel stress or over whelmed I stop and take a good hard look to see if this is in line with the new me.

Your Restarting Checklist

Restarting essentially means creating awareness of what isn't working for you and doing something quickly and effectively to get the good momentum going. It's a reflective practice that goes a long way. These strategies are all excellent for doing straight away without causing you to feel overwhelmed.

– **Book your VIP appointment.** And do it. I mean it, do it. You will create all the energy you need to make your big momentum shift in this one session. Find everything you need for this VIP appointment at www.summersaltlife.com.au/healthyhabits

– **Finish this book.** And take note of all the checklists, highlighting the strategies that you feel will work best for you. You can then plan to incorporate these strategies into your routine during your VIP appointment.

– **Develop a morning routine.** You can incorporate some strategies from the rest of the checklists in this book but consider developing a set routine every morning. The aim is to prepare you mentally, physically and energetically for the day ahead.

– **Complete your time use diary.** Aim to do it for two weeks or five days at a minimum. Do it again after implementing some strategies to see where you have made changes.

– **Incorporate mindfulness into your daily routine**. Stop multi-tasking and focus on one thing at a time. Give it your full attention. For example, at meal times, don't read or watch TV. Give your meal the full attention, taking note of all the sensations you experience.

– **Download a meditation app onto your smart phone.** I state my favourite in the free video, but there's plenty out there. Find one you like and you have access to calming music or voice whenever you need it.

– **See the good in everything.** If you are generally more negative than positive, this is the strategy for you. Find the lesson in the challenges you are facing. You will gain immense appreciation and lessen your likelihood to be so negative in the future.

– **Learn to breathe.** And by breathe, I mean big deep belly-full breathing. Deep breathing is an effective stress management tool so aim to incorporate it regularly throughout your day.

– Start a daily gratitude practice. Every day, record three things you are grateful for. You can either record it in a journal or simply state them in your mind. Incorporate this into your morning routine to start your day on a positive note.

Chapter 3: Refocus

"A life of purpose is the purpose of life" – Oscar Wilde

The fast paced lifestyle of a wonder woman normally means we're too preoccupied with what we're doing instead of why we're doing it. Too often we're caught up in the momentum of doing everything for everyone else but ourselves. Women are amazing at looking after other people's needs and terrible at looking after their own. Funnily enough, we're too busy thinking about others that we don't even consider what our own unique desires and wants in life are.

Knowing your purpose in life can be an overwhelming question to consider. It is however, a very important question to consider. By knowing your very own unique purpose in your life, you are no longer just surviving. You're enabling yourself to thrive. You're essentially enabling yourself to push the boundaries, live a life of your dreams and to do it with inspired action.

The world's most successful entrepreneurs all credit their success to connecting their businesses with their own purposes. The world's happiest people are not necessarily the richest people, but the people who are pursuing their dreams and passions. They are the people who are living every second of their lives in alignment with their purpose. And they are not burdened by stress or negative habits.

Know Your Why

Reconnecting with your purpose enables you to be better equipped for stressful situations. It allows you to make choices that will give you more fulfilment and happiness. More importantly, it enables you to be more confident in your decision making. I have had many women come to me saying that making decisions can be more stressful than the outcome of the decision itself. Decision making is inherently easy once you are consciously aware of your 'Why.'

Your Why is hidden in your values. What you value is what makes up your why. For example, if you value spending time with loved ones, meeting friends over coffee dates or having a jam-packed social calendar, it's fair to say you value friendship and companionship highly.

If you love to create art in your spare time, draw and scribble when you procrastinate or follow the news in the art scene, you could say you creativity is very valuable to you. Doing those things is easy for you – you don't need someone else to motivate you to do those things. Your highest values are played out through all the things you enjoy doing.

As I've already discussed in the Introduction, stress should be seen as a good thing. It enables us to face a challenge at hand. When we pursue the things we love, we are more willing and ready to face all the challenges that come along. Life is never easy and we will always be faced with challenging situations. We are more willing to fight these situations with energy and vigor when it means we'll be a step closer to our dreams or knowing that it will enable us to do the things we enjoy. The term for this is 'inspired action.'

Let me give you an example. You may highly value innovation and entrepreneurship. You may decide to take a big leap of faith and pursue your own business, knowing that it will be tough at first. You know that it's not going to be easy but it is in alignment with your values and Why. Hence, you're taking inspired action towards your purpose.

According to Dr. John Demartini, a human behavioural expert, there is a hierarchy of values. You have your higher values, which are the most important values to you and your lower values, which are the least important.

Busy women can overload their plate with low-valued activities. It's very easy to do – we call them our bad habits! These are the activities that cause you more stress than happiness.

Think about something that you feel forced to do but really don't like doing it. It may be attending a work party or a part of your job that you hate doing. It might be watching television or even cleaning the house. It could even be something that you feel obligated to do – such as going to the gym or supporting your boyfriend at one of his fancy work parties.

It gets a little tough when doing things that would benefit us greatly, such as exercise, is something we consider low on our values list. You may go through this book and decide to vamp up your exercise regime. You give it a good solid crack for a few weeks but then your motivation wanes and before you know it, you haven't been to the gym for months.

If it's low on your value list, you won't do it. Therefore the key is to link the healthy behaviors you're looking to implement, and to tie them to your higher values. What do I mean by that? If, for example, your highest value is to be a loving and engaged mother, you will take inspired action to do whatever it takes to be that loving and engaged mother.

If you're trying to incorporate exercise into your routine, you recognize that getting yourself fit and energetic will help you to have more energy to play with your children. Having more fitness will enable you to keep up with your kids all day long. Once you realize that doing exercise can help you in your quest to be the most loving and engaged mother you can be, you are more likely to do it with ease and less stress.

Social Ideal vs. Your Values

Many people argue that values are simply social ideals in disguise; that they're the social 'expectations' we place on ourselves and each other, and aren't necessarily that important.

I see values as the things we treasure most. Whether that's a trait, activity, feeling, emotion, result, outcome or meaning. They are the things that we place importance on, that make up a collective that we Occupational Therapists like to call 'meaningful occupations.' At the end of the day, it all boils down to what we actually do with our time. But the intentions, feelings, emotions and traits are all part of the equation. The trick though is to recognize that they are truly your values, not somebody else's.

We live in a society where we're ruled by 'The Bigs' – the big corporations in the beauty, food, fashion and pharmaceutical industries, that make big dollars by ensuring we all feel incompetent. They set the agenda for what social idealisms we experience. Culture also plays a significant part in social ideals, religion and tradition inclusive.

They all combine to create a huge range of social ideals that vary according to our experiences with these influences. Sometimes we feel that we should be doing something but in our hearts we know that it's not really what we want to be doing. But it's very, very hard to steer away from that because we feel that we need to live up to those expectations.

It's ultimately up to you to decide if you would rather live your life according to your perceived social ideals or to follow your true passion and desire in life. I truly believe that you, reading this book right now, are a highly driven woman with big dreams. You are capable of pursuing your Why despite any prejudice, barrier or limitations you believe you have.

Finding Your Why

Finding your Why is going to be the most important thing you ever do in your life. We are all innately spiritual beings, whether we consciously accept it or not, and we strive for purpose. The most successful, happy people are the ones who are living in conscious alignment with their purpose. You can see the most successful entrepreneurs touting that their whys are what drove them to success. Businesses are built around a why. That's exactly what mission statement of your business is all about!

Some people have very clear and obvious passions. They know exactly what they want and love to do, and they actively seek to do it as much as possible. Some people, however, find it hard to identify their passion. They see themselves as liking a lot of things but not really having an overwhelming desire or love for anything in particular. It can be disheartening at times because it feels like everything is just mediocre. This can't be further from the truth as once you become consciously aware of your habits, you will uncover your Why. It will be a very liberating experience.

Your Why doesn't need to be spectacular or ground breaking. It simply needs to be exactly what you want to do. If you love to dance for example, you may find that you're happy attending weekly dance lessons and attending musicals. Alternatively, you may desire to make dancing you day job, whether it be a dancer, teacher, or running dance tours in your local city. You may highly value your role as a mother and don't have a drive to create a successful career or to be in the spotlight. Keep in mind that when you live your life in alignment to being the best mother you can be, you are no less successful than the millionaire entrepreneur. Success is defined entirely by you.

The Power of Visualization

You might find in your quest to finding your Why that you spend a lot of time visualizing what you want. The art of visualization is actually very powerful. I've worked in the public mental health system for a number of years and it continues to amaze me how often my clients wouldn't even consider what they wanted, yet alone visualized their deepest desires. They struggled to take any inspired action, because they hadn't even visualized their end desire to know what action to take! They don't see their future as bright, which ultimately means their future will not be bright.

Visualization is about creating all the images, sounds and feelings in your mind surrounding an activity in order to practice in a perfect environment. Visualization is a great tool for athletes or even those wanting to lose weight (The Jon Gabriel Method places huge emphasis on visualization). The reason why visualization works is because you are strengthening the paths for that skill in your brain. Your mind doesn't even notice the difference, so practicing this way during those times where you are away from your practice environment can truly help you improve. An Australian psychologist, Alan Richardson did a little experiment on visualization with a group of basketball players. He divided them in 3 groups and tested each player's ability to make free throws. The first group would practice 20 minutes every day, the second group would only visualize themselves making free throws without real practice and the third group would not practice or visualize. The results will surprise you. There was significant improvement on the group that only visualized; they were almost as good as they guys who actually practiced.

In terms of creating your best life where you are no longer crippled by stress, you are essentially training your mind to stress better. As I'm sure that whatever you are visualizing, you won't be visualizing you being crippled by stress!

A good exercise to do is to visualize your best day. What would you be doing, where would you be and who would you be with? There are no limits to this activity. You have no money, time or travel limits – visualize your most amazing day girl! Secondly, visualize your ideal working day. What hours would you work, what would you be working on, how would you be working, who would you be working with and so on. Again, there are no limits. To give you an example, my dream working day would go something like this:

– Up at 6am for a workout with a personal trainer, followed by a beach swim.

– A homemade healthy breakfast with a green smoothie, sitting on my deck with a view of the ocean.

– Head to my home office and check emails, get my daily list out and delegate tasks to my assistant.

– Work 2-3 hours on creating virtual programs, blogging, writing, researching and other creative pursuits.

– Lunch at home or a visit to my favorite local organic café.

– Afternoon dedicated to relationships whether they be coaching, networking or events.

– Official work day over by 3 or 4pm, leaving the evening to do whatever I please.

Your dream working day may be completely different and I expect it would be very much so. Whatever it is, visualize it clearly and visualize it regularly.

Even better, create a visual inspiration board (see your Refocusing Checklist). By visualizing this daily you're reminding yourself of your highest values and creating a future you want. Inspired action always follows visualization when it is in alignment with your true values.

What to do When You're Out of Whack

Stress prevails long and hard when we work against our purpose. I truly believe chronic, ongoing stress is a warning sign from our bodies to let us know we are out of whack with our

Why. Knowing your Why is the first step. Living your why is the next step. And boy, it's a crucial step.

The best and easiest thing you can do right now is to start questioning 'Why!?' for every little thing you do. You absolutely should do this every time you feel the burden of unrelenting stress.

In your VIP appointment, you will look over how you spend your time and what is your attitude towards life and stress. You may notice in this appointment that you reflect a lot on the choices you make and how they impact on you. This combined with the themes you find will give you an insight into your values hierarchy.

Remember this, you are more likely to use stress better when you're consciously aware of your Why. Anything that you do that is challenging or stress-provoking will become easier as you see that it's a necessary step towards fulfilling your purpose.

Real Women, Real Stories

Shakti Grace, of The Holistic Chef

The last 2 years, and especially 12 months, have seen my body and mental state really show the results of periods of endured chronic stress. Adrenal Fatigue and Thyroid issues and overall hormone disruption. The whole time this has been building, I kept doing my best to ignore the reality of it all, and keep being the one woman "machine", "force of nature" I have been told I present as. The last laugh is only on me as blood tests and observations of our nearest and dearest don't lie. The irony of teaching people how to live well and mindfully is not lost on me at all. That being said we are also our own greatest teachers, and these lessons come to serve us well if we choose to heed them.

Most recently, I went back to sit at the Vipassana Meditation 10-day silent course, this is the most profoundly amazing way to drop back into your body, quieten the mind, calm the adrenals, and reconnect with a strong and solid meditation technique. No technology, no food after 12 noon, no talking and lots of meditation. I am amazed how quickly I could see the craziness of my life. I continue to meditate at least one hour, sometimes two, a day. I find Vipassana for me to be the best way to be reminded of the clinging, craving, aversion, misery cycle, and find that the teaching of equanimity.

To sit on the grass below the trees, feel the sun on my face, listen to the birds, hug a tree, and especially swim daily in the ocean - these save me on all levels of my being, and bring me back into a state of equanimity and also offer big opportunities to practice another thing that is important.

The simple things that I am so deeply grateful for are vital to my aliveness and energy. When I sit down before each meal and give gratitude, gaze up at the sky, swim in the ocean, look at the happy face of the doggies that live on my property, give thanks for the food I grow as I harvest it for a meal, visit with a friend, read a letter from a loved one.

My adrenals love staying up late! They don't really but they have been in that adrenal cycle of going past the bodies signals and pushing through. Sleep at reasonable time and for a solid amount of time is what I am committed to this year.

Nutritious, soothing, nourishing food is also important. It's a part of what i do in my life purpose and what I require to keep my body and spirit healthy, so it is a no brainer for me

I am my own worst enemy when the stress levels get too high. I am also taking a stance on this by offering positivity to myself

daily in a conscious way, focusing on the things I am achieving day by day that uplift and support, this is nurture at the soul level along with all other practices mentioned.

Your Refocusing Checklist

If you do nothing else, do this. Your Why is going to be the biggest and most important factor in improving your life. You immediately eliminate a lot of stressors when you truly live in alignment with your purpose.

    – Look at your time use diary. Take note of all the things you were doing that didn't require external motivation. The things most important to you come to you easily. Notice any themes that arise. You should have done this in your VIP appointment already.

    – Set your intentions. Do this regularly and make it a healthy habit to check in. Setting yearly intentions are great, monthly are even better. Intentions are the things you want to achieve. Your Why will be the driving force behind.

    – Set a daily priority list. List three things every day that you must get done. Aim to get these done before 11am if possible. This will free you up to focus on less important things later on the day, instead of feeling stressed that you haven't done what you need and want to do.

    – Create a vision board. Vision, or inspirational boards, are brilliant at giving you a visual reminder at what you are striving for. Add photos and pictures from magazines, inspiring quotes and whatever takes your fancy. The key is that they all have to visual represent your why and the things you want to do.

    – **Practice the art of manifesting**. Create positive statements of the things you want to manifest. For example, 'I am going to take a holiday to Byron Bay this year.' Don't say 'I might' or 'I hope to' – have firm, confident statements about what you want exactly. The word 'someday' is one of the most dangerous words in the dictionary.

    – **Create a vision statement for your life.** Much like a business, create a vision or mission statement that applies to your life. Revisit and reshape this statement as your values change

    – **Take inspired action.** Start implementing the things you need to do in order to live in alignment with your purpose. Think, "What do I need to do now to get where I want to be?"

Chapter 4: Renourish

"The food you eat can be either the safest and most powerful form of medicine, or the slowest form of poison." - Ann Wigmore

---

Take-away can be a busy woman's best friend. In the time-sense, maybe, but for your health and well-being? Not a chance!

It's very cliché, but having a healthy diet is extremely important when it comes to managing your stress. You cannot function effectively if you do not fuel your body right. When you fuel your body, you're also fuelling your mind.

Most busy women are naturally health-conscious. They seek to eat well and move well. The problem is the flurry of misinformation out there. There are fad diets left, right and centre. You can find information telling you to not eat something but also to eat it.

Navigating the wellness world can be stressful in itself. I'm going to make it easier for you. What you need to know to prepare your body to beat your stress is right here.

Forget Calories, Focus On Ingredients.

Here's something for you – stop calorie counting. The number one thing you need to do in relation to their diet is to forget the whole concept of calories. They're the least important factor when it comes to your diet. Seriously! The ingredients of your food have a greater impact on your wellbeing than the amount of calories.

Have a look at the last packaged food you ate. What was on the ingredient list? Are there names you can't pronounce? If you cannot pronounce an ingredient, the chances your body recognizing that ingredient is slim to none.

The food industry has bombarded us with products that are food-like. They then slap on a 'healthy' marketing message to entice you to purchase their product. Because you're a health-conscious woman, you buy those products thinking that you're doing yourself and your family a favor. Food-like products are not healthy. Real, natural, unprocessed food is the only healthy food you're ever going to come across.

Eat Real Food

'Real food' is food that's as close as possible to its natural state. They have no added chemical preservatives, flavorings or colors. There are no numbers listed in the ingredients and nothing man-made is added.

Here is a list of generalized examples of what real food can include. Keep in mind that organic is the gold standard.

– Fresh fruit and vegetables.

– Dried fruit without preservatives.

– Pastured, free-range, ethical meats.

– Sustainably caught fish.

– Raw nuts and seeds.

– Coconut, olive and nut oils (Note: vegetable oils are not real food!)

– Grass-fed full fat dairy products, such as milk, yoghurt and cheeses, from cow, goat, sheep, or buffalo.

– Whole-grains and pseudo-grains (preferably gluten-free)such as quinoa and buckwheat.

–'Superfoods' such as spirulina, chlorella, seaweed, maca.

–Teas and coffees.

You will be able to find 'non-real food' versions of all these foods in your supermarket. Instead of spending your time looking at the calorie list or the fats-carbs-protein ratios, learn to read the ingredient list first. Everything you need to know is listed in the ingredients list!

Obviously, this will eliminate a lot of the foods you find at your local supermarket. In fact, you'll notice that you'll only really find any real food on the periphery of the supermarket – all the junk lies in the central aisles and there's a very good reason for this. Real food is perishable – it doesn't last for years on a supermarket shelf. Therefore the turnover of real food is a lot quicker, hence why they're located on the outskirts of the supermarket.

Turning onto a real food diet will ultimately mean that you will need to cook and prepare most of your food. There are some great cafes, restaurants and food delivery services that offer real food options but you'll need to do your research for your local options. The good news is that it's a growing industry and I expect it will become easier to find quick and easy real food options. In the meantime, look at your regular diet and find a healthier, real food alternative for your main meals.

Avoid These as Much as You Can

There are some types of food that are best avoided as much as possible. They do nothing but create a plethora of ill-health for our bodies and our minds.

Trans Fats

Trans fats are the man-made fats found in many processed foods. Virtually any product that comes from a factory will have trans fat. Trans fats damage cells, increase inflammation, and interrupt normal brain function. The biggest problem here is that it interrupts our brain function – it literally interrupts our ability to stress effectively. These are mind-altering substances. Their effects are slow and gradual, and will cause a host of serious health problems for you if you continue to have them in your diet.

Trans fats are generally found in baked goods, vegetable oils, margarine, fried foods, frozen dinners and snack foods. If you grab any of these foods in the supermarket and it claims to be '0 trans fats,' it technically isn't. Legally yes, because producers can label it as '0 trans fats' if it's below 0.5grams per serving. You know they include trans fats when you see any ingredients listed with 'partially hydrogenated.' The best thing to do is to avoid these products completely and make your own healthy, real food versions instead.

The Fat Myth

There are hundreds and thousands of myths floating around cyberspace when it comes to food. The reality is that what we currently know about nutrition is only a small glimpse of the whole picture. There is more and more information coming out every day and scientists are constantly finding new information that throws what we know out the window. The latest myth-buster that you must be aware of is saturated fats.

Saturated fats have been demonized since the 1970s due to some very poor research and excellent scare campaigning which bred a generation living off low-fat products. We've been told that eating low fat is going to make you skinnier and healthier. In fact, it's doing more harm than good. Our bodies, particularly our nervous system, rely on the so-called 'dreaded' saturated fats to function effectively.

Low fat products are a double whammy. When you take the fat out, you take the flavor out. To make up for it, food producers add our favourite toxin, sugar. Essentially, we're trading in a vital ingredient for a highly addictive toxic substance. Great for the food industry, not so great for you.

Do not fear saturated fats. Monounsaturated fats are the healthiest fats you can find and saturated fats are not far behind. They will not clog your arteries or raise your cholesterol. Don't believe me? A meta-analysis by the Journal of Clinical Nutrition, of the results of 21 studies that followed more than 347,000 total participants for up to 23 years showed that "there is no significant evidence for concluding that dietary saturated fats is associated with an increased risk of coronary heart disease, stroke or cardiovascular disease." Go on, enjoy that butter.

Refined Sugars And Artificial Sweeteners

Sweet, glorious, devilish sugar! It's the crack of the food industry. Highly addictive, beautifully sweet, and incredibly toxic.

Sugar, in particularly high-fructose corn syrup for Americans or table sugar for Australians, promotes obesity, leads to diabetes, inflames the brain and is as clinically addictive as cocaine. High sugar consumption is also tied to a host of mental disorders such as lowering IQ, anxiety, ADHD, eating disorders, fatigue, learning difficulties and hyperactivity.

You may think you don't eat much sugar if you don't drink soft drinks, eat cakes or sweets or even add sugar to your coffee. But the reality is that sugar is in every single processed food item on the supermarket shelf. Sugar masquerades behind a range of scientific sounding names, such as barley malt, beet sugar, brown sugar, buttered syrup, cane-juice crystals, cane sugar, caramel, high fructose corn syrup, and any word ending in –ose such as dextrose or sucrose. You will be hard-pressed to find many foods without any sugar in them.

Artificial sweeteners are no better either. Aspartame, the artificial sweetener found in your favourite diet soft drink, is the technical name for Equal and NutraSweet and probably the most common and most controversial of all the artificial sweeteners.

In America, aspartame accounts for over 75 percent of the adverse reactions to food additives reported to the FDA and many of these reactions are very serious, including seizures and death. Other symptoms being caused by aspartame include dizziness, headaches, migraines, weight gain, memory loss and fatigue.

Aspartame is bad news. If you are a fan of your Berocca, you may want to double check the ingredient list.

Gluten

The modern diet tends to promote wheat-based foods for breakfast, lunch and dinner. Typical snacks are also heavily wheat-based. We're quite literally consuming considerable amounts of a gluten, a protein shown to cause localized inflammation in the gut.

There's a growing body of research showing how harmful gluten-containing grains are to our health. Research now shows that the intestinal damage of celiac disease occurs in at least 1 in 100 people and the numbers of celiac-affected people has quadrupled over the last fifty years.

I have come across very few people who tolerate gluten well. And it seems like I'm not the only one who thinks that. Whilst it is still controversial, there is growing evidence that it isn't just those with celiac disease that are experiencing the damaging symptoms of gluten. An increasing numbers of physicians have come to the conclusion that gluten is potentially harmful for everyone. Professor Alessio Fasano, a leading researcher in celiac disease, states that no one can digest gluten and that gluten sensitivity affects millions of people.

Gluten is ultimately inflammatory. Inflammation causes havoc in our bodies, leading to a myriad of condition and diseases, such as diabetes, muscle and joint pain, arthritis, and leaky gut. There is emerging evidence of the gut-mind connection and there is a view that the gut is the 'second brain.' When our guts are broken and beaten, our brains are paying dearly for it. This is not good news for those wanting to stress better and live long, happy lives.

If you're not quite willing to give up your bread, at least get tested to see if you're sensitive to gluten. Short of going to the doctor and getting tested for celiac, the best thing to do is to go completely gluten-free for 30 days then reintroduce it into your diet. Take note of any effects, such as headache, runny nose, bloating, gas, or simple discomfort. I'd be surprised if you didn't notice anything wayward, but if you're one of the lucky ones, you may decide to continue gluten in your diet. That's completely up to you but I want to highlight how important it is to minimize it in your diet. There is nothing healthy about gluten-containing foods. You should aim to be nourished from your foods and gluten-containing foods offer no needed nourishment in your diet.

A Word on Alcohol

A hard day can leave us feeling beat. A glass of wine can really take the edge off. Hardworking women are one of the groups with the highest risk of developing binge drinking or alcoholism. These disorders are not good news for our health or our stress management. In fact, they aren't good news full stop.

Alcohol depletes our mood-boosting B vitamins and slows down our brain metabolism. Alcohol is also acutely neurotoxic. It alters the normal activity of the nervous system, damages neurons and may cause damage to nervous tissues. This is not the outcome we are looking for when we're trying to manage our stress more effectively.

It's completely up to you if you want to abstain from alcohol for good or not. If you do choose to have alcohol in your diet, keep in mind your reasons for drinking your favourite drop. Alcohol is not an effective stress management tool. It goes against you body's natural stress mechanisms, hence causing problems.

Find a healthier alternative for that glass of red when you get home, such as a pot of herbal tea or relaxing, meditative exercise like yoga. Enjoy alcohol when the occasion calls for it, not when the stress begs for it.

Your Unique Diet

Whilst I have supplied some recommendations of what to change in your diet, I simply cannot give you an exact outline or plan of what your diet should be.

There is no 'one size fits all' approach to diets. We all come in different shapes and sizes, activity patterns, preferences, tolerances and histories, all of which influence the most effective diet for ourselves.

Furthermore, our diets change all the time. Our needs change as we grow older, our activity patterns change, when we become ill with the flu or even when we become pregnant. Thus, it's important to learn how to eat intuitively.

Intuitive Eating

Emotional eating is the bane for many wonder women. Comfort foods give us instant relief when we're feeling highly strung.

But did you know that stress affects the activation of reward pathways and impairs your attempts to control your eating? So basically it makes it harder for us to resist our cravings, which are almost always sugary, fatty, salty foods. And there is a biological reason for these cravings – highly palatable foods give us instant pleasure, activating the dopamine and opioid pathways in the brain. Then to make it even more of a nightmare for us, a stressed brain expresses both a strong drive to eat and an impaired ability to stop eating. So not only do we want to eat unhealthy foods, we literally can't stop gorging on them!

Intuitive eating is going back to our roots and approaching food with a loving, stress free relationship.

Children are brilliant intuitive eaters. They only eat when they're hungry and reject food once they've had enough. They're not yet tainted by other reasons for eating food and they haven't yet been taught how to us food as a coping mechanism. As we grow older, we encounter the food myths and become engrossed in a culture of dieting. Children, who are yet to experience this, simply listen to their own body cues. They eat when they're hungry and they stop when they're full. Forcing a child to finish all the food on their plate when they've had enough is actually quite counterproductive and one of the first food myths we face.

Our bodies know when we have eaten enough food. We make it hard for ourselves when we use food as rewards or relief from stress. It goes against the concept of intuitive eating.

When we don't eat intuitively, we eat too much or too little. We eat the types of foods that our bodies don't like. We eat because we're bored, restless, tired, emotional or because your friends are peer pressuring you to eat that tray of sandwiches.

This results in weight gain, physical discomfort, feeling guilty and cultivates a negative attitude towards food. Therefore it is really important to eat meals in a relaxed state, not when we are driving to work, talking on the phone and worried about being late for a meeting with the big boss.

Real Women, Real Stories

Sally-Ann Blanshard, of Nourish Coaching

As a mum to a 2 and 4 year old, a wife to a 41 year old and owner of a 2 year old business, I was continually putting their needs ahead of my own. 2013 was my year of change and, put simply, enough was enough. I felt out of whack and exhausted in many areas of life. I chose a word for the year - Commitment. I needed to give focus and energy to each area of my life while also prioritizing me and in turn lightening my load.

I changed my working days to a back to back three days and made sure on the two days I did not work, I had mummy time with my children. Mummy time was to be rich in experiences and activities. Memory making moments as I call them! Some days we baked cupcakes for our afternoon picnic in the garden; others took a ferry on the river and had adventures.

The result here was children that knew when I had their time - I made time for them and only them. No work.

In regards to relationships, I implemented date night and made sure that we had time for one another as well as time for our own personal interests. This created more sense of balance and personal identity - not just being mum and dad.

By working 3 days back to back, I could actually think more seamlessly. I could guide my clients to work with me on the days and times I had available and not feel guilty about not being free on my 'mummy' days. As I move into 2014, I will now be working on 4 days a week. This has really helped me amplify

 how I operate in business and simplify my process and structure to work more effectively.

Last year was huge in terms of hitting reset for me in relation to my health and fitness. If I was to thrive in the role of parent, wife and business owner I needed to feed myself well and move more. I started to eat clean by avoiding processed foods and increased my fitness activities with running, swimming and classes at the gym.

I am six months into this commitment and the results are incredible in terms of how my skin feels, my mood, my energy, confidence and my capacity to engage in all the roles have. I can now do that at an optimal level.

People often ask how I do it all - but I just say - this is my version of busy - and I am committed

Your Renourishing Checklist

You want to nourish your body as best as you can. It will help you to stress better, ward off disease and infection, and feel better. Your health is your number one priority. If you choose to continue eating unhealthy food, you will become sick. It is the accumulation of a poor diet that is our downfall. That said, don't feel guilty about the occasional indulgence.

Our bodies are fabulous healing machines and are capable of recovering very quickly when they're looked after most of the time. The guilt you may feel from eating that block of chocolate will cause you more harm than the chocolate itself!

These strategies will help you get started on your journey to a healthier diet.

– **Add more good stuff**. Don't worry too much about cutting out the bad foods to begin with, particularly if you don't feel ready to do so. The feeling of deprivation will mean that it won't last. Instead, focus on adding nourishing foods to your diet. Aim to have vegetables at every main meal. Eventually, you will crowd out all the bad foods.

– **Find healthier alternatives for your favourite foods.** We all tend to have 5-10 meals that make up our core staples. Instead of eliminating them for good (that is a recipe for failure!), 'healthify' them. Add more vegetables, replace processed ingredients with a homemade version and make it gluten-free.

– **Have breakfast, and make it hearty.** Breakfast really is the most important meal of the day. But fuelling up on sugar-laden cereals or wheat-loaded toast is not a good start. Have a high protein breakfast that will keep you full for longer. You won't get the mid-morning slump either as the slow-releasing energy will sustain you for hours.

    – **Keep it simple**. You don't need to do fancy recipes to be healthy. Simple is best and easiest. Get creative in the kitchen when you get bored with your standard meals or whenever the creative juices are flowing. Just don't feel like you need to be the next Jamie Oliver to be healthy.

    – **Cook larger meals**: Cook a huge batch of your favourite meal and divide it into smaller portions for later. You can place them in the freezer for those nights you're running late or can't be bothered cooking. Spaghetti Bolognese (with gluten-free noodles), casseroles and curries are great for this. You could even make large portion of salads and divide them up for lunch during the week.

    – **Get a slow cooker**: Simply place a range of vegetables, meat and seasonings into a slow-cooker before you head off to work. By the time you get home, you have a delicious meal ready to go. Not to mention the amazing smell that will greet you.

    – **Practice intuitive eating**. Eat mindfully at every meal. Avoid eating on the go and schedule in time every day to sit down and enjoy your meal. Eat slowly to allow your satiety cues to hit your brain before you eat too much! Don't eat just because it's 'time' to eat either. If you're not hungry at lunch time, eat a later when you are.

    – **Sit down and eat**. Avoid eating in the car or on the go, as this goes against intuitive eating principles. Schedule in the time if you find you're always rushing about and eating on the go.

Chapter 5: Re-energize

"Training gives us an outlet for suppressed energies created by stress

and thus tones the sprit just as exercise conditions the body."

- Arnold Schwarnzenegger

Your body doesn't just need good fuel. It needs to move. A lot of busy women are sitting at a desk for 8-9 hours a day, then sitting in a car or public transport for another hour or so, then going home and sitting in front of the TV or computer for another hour or more after that. Finally we go to bed.

Our bodies are not made to be sitting down for most of the day. Our bodies are made to move regularly and consistently.

Move It

Moving our bodies equips us to be energetic. It breeds energy. When we're energetic, we're able to handle stressful situations with aplomb. Our thinking is clearer, our attention is sharp. Our bodies become our fighting tool in our daily busyness. In fact, it's our best tool to fight the stress hormones.

In Chapter 2 we discussed how our innate physiological stress response is activated in response to a perceived threat. This response lets out a flurry of stress hormones, such as cortisol, adrenalin and oxytocin. These hormones are problematic when there is excess levels of them in the blood. The only way to 'burn' the hormones when they are released is to exercise.

If you think about it, it's a great evolutionary tool. You're faced with a threat, your body activates its survival mechanism and releases a torrent of chemicals that will energise your body as quickly as possible. You then have the energy to get away from the threat. As soon as your safe, your body returns to a relax state. It is in that 'run for your life' phase that the hormones are doing their job and burning off.

In today's world, we are facing threats that don't require us to physically move. The hormones are released but they aren't getting used. Instead, they are just circulating in your blood stream. With this understanding, we know that exercise is an excellent tool for stressing better.

The exercise to burn your stress hormones doesn't need to be strenuous either. You simply need a break a sweat. Dropping to the floor and doing 30 push-ups will be enough to break down the stress hormones and leave you feeling better.

This also goes for your general exercise routine. You don't need to train like an athlete to reap the benefits. Creating a routine where you simply move your body every day is going to do wonders for your physical and emotional health. Research consistently shows that your chances of getting serious health disorders such as cancer, diabetes, stroke, arthritis, osteoporosis and many more, are decreased with regular physical activity. Mental health also benefits from regular exercise too.

It can be hard for the working woman to fit exercise into their daily schedule. The good news is that you don't need to do all your exercise in one big hit to reap the benefits. Doing smaller bouts of exercise throughout the day is just as beneficial.

In my non-scientific, personal view, this is a better option anyway. We are constantly faced with stressors throughout the day therefore we are more likely releasing stress hormones numerous times during the day. Surely it is more beneficial to have sporadic bouts of movement to keep the level of these hormones in our blood stream low, than it is to do one big session in the morning? Much like your diet, your exercise routine is going to be very unique and tailored to your individual circumstances. There will be no 'fitness plan fits all.'

Work Hard, Play Harder

Exercise doesn't have to be a dreaded chore. In fact, it should be fun and playful. Growing up and entering the fast-paced career world means we lose sight of the glorious concept of play. Play is all about having fun. It's about exploring your world in a whole new way that enriches all of your senses.

Have you noticed how much children move about when they are playing? Granted, video games and TV are creating a culture of still and unfit kids, but generally speaking, kids are highly active and moving their bodies when they're playing. They swing on the monkey bars, climb over things, run around aimlessly and carry objects around. They exercise without knowing it.

Adults don't do that anymore, particularly women. We feel like we have to act proper and be socially acceptable at all times. Running around aimlessly, or spontaneously doing cartwheels, just doesn't seem appropriate. It's a shame really because we're missing out on exercise and a whole lot of spontaneous fun.

The thought of going to a gym can be horrifying for some. If you're one of the people that the sheer thought of exercise is a total nightmare, finding active fun things to do may be more your cup of tea. You could go to dancing classes, cooking workshops, volunteer at an animal shelter or babysit your sister's kids. You are more likely to do the activity if the fitness element is only a secondary gain. You will be so focused on enjoying yourself and having fun that you don't realize that you're working up a sweat!

Rest is Important Too

As with everything, it's all about balance. We need to move our bodies frequently and consistently, and we need to rest our bodies in much the same way. Rest allows our body to recovery from daily stressors.

Sitting on the couch watching TV or sitting at the desk does not count as rest. The simple reason is that your body and mind are still active. Notice the next time you're sitting at your desk how tense your muscles are. You may notice that you're tensing your shoulders or your stomach.

Notice the next time you're watching a movie how your muscles almost mimic what is happening on the screen. Action and horror movies are great at causing us to tense our bodies in anticipation of what is going to happen next. We may think we are relaxing and enjoying the show when in fact our bodies are subconsciously reacting to the stimuli!

Real rest is essentially relaxing our body and mind in complete stillness. It is much like being mindful, which we discussed in Chapter 3. It is about completely centering your body and mind into the present moment.

Meditation as a Healing Tool

Meditation is the second most effective tool behind sleep to relax your body. We spoke about mindfulness and meditation in Chapter 3, particularly how valuable it is in bringing us to the present moment. But it is also very effective in promoting the body to recover and reenergize.

Meditation has been scientifically proven to activate the relaxation response. Almost every health condition improves as a result. In his research at Harvard, Herbert Benson demonstrated that meditation is effective in allergic skin reactions, anxiety, mild to moderate depression, asthma, herpes, diabetes, fatigue, hypertension, infertility, insomnia, and all forms of pain such as backaches, headaches, abdominal pain, muscle pain, and joint aches.

Much like exercise, meditation has been shown to decrease stress-related cortisol, reduce our heart rate, increase blood flow in the brain, strengthen the immune system, and lead to a state of relaxation.

Dr. Herbert Benson, a Harvard Professor defines meditation in his book 'The Relaxation Response' as:

"Repetition of a word, sound, phrase, prayer, or muscular activity while passively disregarding everyday thoughts that inevitably come to mind and returning to your repetition."

Note: You could argue that this definition is the scientific version of the 'New Age' definition I mentioned in Chapter 1. Either way, they mean the same thing.

Dr. Benson is essentially saying that exercise could be considered a form of meditation. If you think about it, it really is. Athletes talk about 'being in the zone' when they're exercising or playing their sport. They're talking about being in a highly effective frame of mind where they're intently focused on their task at hand without distraction. This is a meditative state!

As I mentioned above, exercise is highly effective at burning off the excess stress hormones. A meditative exercise is going to be extremely effective at helping deactivate the stress response.

Like everything, it's always about the balance and finding what works best for you. You may find that regular exercise coupled with regular meditation is your best option. Or you might prefer to do a lot more exercise and less meditation. Whatever works best for you, you need to find it and make it your routine. A little of bit exercise and meditation can go a long way in managing your stress.

Don't Skimp On The Sleep

There's no better stress management tool than a good ol' snooze. Your body and mind use this precious time to heal and recover from our daily grind. Research has shown that sleep can help improve our memories, reduce inflammation, improve attention and concentration, maintain a healthy weight and even contribute to longer lifespan. Take notice of the difference you have after a good night's sleep versus a bad night's sleep. They're quite stark aren't they?

The average person should be aiming for 8-9 hours' sleep a night. Mums get it tough considering they have a very real and valid reason for their interrupted sleep. But for those who don't have the shrill cry of a newborn interrupting their sleep, they should be sleeping long and deep every night.

Experts say that over 80% of the population are sleep deprived. Long working hours, high stress levels, poor health and various sleeping disorders are all culprits. Other factors that may compound our sleeping efforts may include poor diets, bright light exposure after sunset (such as computers and TVs) and poor bedroom environments (such as noise exposure, poor bedding, and poor ventilation). Good sleep hygiene is necessary for a good night's sleep.

Chronic stress can interfere with our sleep, particularly if we're really good at brewing over things in our minds. The endless mind chatter can delay falling asleep as well as waking us up throughout the night. In Chapter 7, I explain how you can gain control over this chatter.

You will also find that your sleep will improve the better you are at stressing. You will sleep long and well if you apply small changes in each area of the Re-approach to stress. That said, these things take time to develop, so it's important to prioritize sleep. You need to make time for it. Simple as that.

When you do your time use diary and notice that you're wasting time on low value activities, the first thing you should be doing is scheduling any extra time for sleep. This is a must for those who are getting less than eight hours of sleep a night.

Real Women, Real Stories

Elise Carver, of Little Bantam Fitness

Being so driven makes it hard not to get stressed out over all the little things like money, relationships, what your next move is, whether you will be successful or not. It's a part of life. and no matter how much I tell myself that it's just concern or

I'm "thinking about it, that's all" the truth is every minute I dwell on the future is one more point in the stress department!

I believe the best way to manage stress is ensure your body is in balance state. This doesn't mean REALLY relaxed or REALLY calm after all if we didn't get excited and pumped up we wouldn't have the mental energy to get through the day. I'm referring to a balanced routine.

For me the best way to achieve this is first and foremost getting plenty of SLEEP! Without the proper rest your body and your mind cannot sort out and recover from the days adventures. I also like to go to bed at a set time to read myself to sleep and wake up at a set time to start my day by walking the dogs. Getting the body moving first thing is great for moving out of sleepy mode and building up an appetite!

Starting the day with a healthy breakfast to give you energy will help you cope with life's little and big dilemma's. Spoil yourself with a decent bowl of muesli or scrambled eggs and Avo! Also keep in mind light meals at night (avoid pasta, potatoes & lots of meat) make for easy digestion and better sleep patterns.

If you have a spare 20 – 30 mins I find it always helps to quiet the mind and release the body by doing Yoga or simples stretches holding each for 30 seconds. Think of it as your "defrag" time!

Your Re-Energizing Checklist

You don't need to be an athlete to be healthy. You simply need to move every single day. Ideally 30 minutes at an absolute minimum but the key is to move every single day in any possible way. On the other end of the spectrum, it's important to take time to properly rest. This includes sleep and/or forms of meditation. Remember, a little goes a long way.

– **Find a form of exercise that is fun.** If you hate running, don't do it. Hate the gym? Don't sign up. Love walking the dog? Have fun! Moving your body should be enjoyable. You are causing yourself undue pressure when you feel obliged to follow conventional fitness methods.

– **Exercise without knowing it.** Short of joining a gym or hiring a personal trainer, you can easily incorporate more movement into your daily routine with a little creative thinking. Walk to the shops, carry heavy bags, ride to work. Be creative.

– **Ride or walk to work.** Ditch the car and try old fashioned modes of transportation when travelling to work or someplace close. Need to pick up a bottle of milk? Why don't you walk instead? If you do have to drive to work, consider parking your car a few blocks away and walking the rest. Parking at the far corner of a supermarket car park also encourages incidental exercise. Don't have time? Even better, more motivation to up the pace!

– **Encourage walking meetings.** Why not take a different tack and instead of holding your meetings in your drab meeting room, take the crew for a walk down the street. A change of scenery can really boost productivity as well as lift you and your colleagues' spirits.

– **Take your lunch break elsewhere**. Firstly, take your lunch break. Every day. You are never too busy to eat and take a break. Secondly, take it out of the office or home. Walk down the street to stretch your legs and get some vitamin d. It will help you feel recharged and reenergised, encouraging more productivity when you get back to the office.

– **Consider a stand up desk**. These things are crazy great. Doing your work whilst standing up creates amazing productivity. When sitting, we tend to slouch around and get into a comfortable mode. When standing, you're more attentive to your task at hand and more likely to get your work done in less time. Not to mention that standing does a lot more wonders for you booty than sitting does.

– **Move with the girls**. We all love to catch up with our sisters over a coffee. Why not turn it into a short walk? You could end up at your favourite café to make it a double whammy.

– **Look at it as movement, not exercise**. Some of us cringe with fear at the word exercise and can stir up traumatic memories of those rainy, cold mornings at boot camp being yelled at by that hunk of a trainer. Change your mind set to see it simply as 'moving.' You're more likely to keep it up and incorporate it into your routine with this mindset.

– Practice mindfulness or meditation whenever you can. On the train, in the car, shower, even in the elevator. You don't have to be sitting on a luscious green lawn with your legs crossed for an hour in glorious sunshine to experience the benefits of meditation. Take ten big deep breaths and focus on these at any chance you get.

– Create a stress hormone buster tool kit. Create a list of exercises that are guaranteed to break a sweat and don't need any equipment at all. Push ups, sit ups, star jumps and burpees are great examples. Every time you feel you are under a 'stress attack,' do twenty of an exercise on that list.

Chapter 6: Rethink

"Watch your thoughts; they become words.

Watch your words; they become actions.

Watch your actions; they become habit.

Watch your habits; they become character.

Watch your character; it becomes your destiny" – Lao Tzu

The thoughts going through our heads have tremendous power. We don't realize exactly how powerful they are. Remember back to a time when you were stressed out: were your thoughts negative or positive? They were negative right? When we're stressed, we tend to go into problem-solving mode, seeking out all the problems in order to figure out a solution. It becomes a vicious circle and we get caught up going over and over the possibilities in our head.

You are Not Your Thoughts

There are many names for the talk going on in our heads. Some call it the ego, mean girl, self-talk, mind chatter, or simply the voice in their head. We have a natural tendency to get caught up in our thoughts. Remember those times when you've drifted off with the fairies, without a clue as to what's happening around you? We also have a tendency to believe everything our mind says. Because we know it all right? The truth is, we simply get caught up in the story.

Our self-talk is likely to take a negative tone most of the time. It's completely normal. In fact, it's a survival mechanism. Think about it, back in the day we would not have survived if we thought that big furry lion was cute. Our brains are problem-solving machines and see everything as a potential threat to our livelihood. So we are actually hard-wired to be negative Nellie's – we're never going to get rid of this natural tendency. We will forever experience negative thoughts. It's how we manage those thoughts that matters most in managing our stress and cultivating healthy habits.

Thinking Styles

There are a range of thinking styles that aren't very conducive to managing our stress better. These are the negative habits of your mind. Read the descriptions below and find if any sounds like you. You may notice you have a dominant thinking style or that you have a combination of a few.

– **Black and white thinking**. Tend to see things in 'black' or 'white' and with no shades of grey. It is a tendency to see things as good or bad, not a combination of both.

– **Mental filter**. This is when you apply a certain filter to the evidence before you. For example, you may only notice your failures or shortcomings without seeing your successes.

– **Over generalizing**. You create patterns from single events, thinking that since it applied to that event, it will apply to all events. It's also applying any conclusion you come up with to a much broader landscape.

– **Magnifying and minimizing**. Blowing things out of proportion and minimizing something else to make it seem less important.

- **Emotional reasoning**. You feel a certain emotion and conclude that because you're feeling that way, it must be true. For example, maybe you feel embarrassed. You then reason you must have done something wrong.

– **Should**. When we tell ourselves that we 'should' or 'ought' to be doing something, we generate feelings of frustration and guilt, or even a sense of failure.

– **Labelling**. Assigning a label to others and ourselves can be very unhelpful and limiting. For example, 'I'm an anxiety sufferer' creates an attachment to suffering from anxiety, which in turn promotes anxious behaviours.

– **Personalization.** This is when you blame yourself for something that wasn't entirely your fault.

– **Mind reading**. We think we know exactly what other people are thinking.

All these thinking styles are unhelpful thinking styles. They promote and encourage stress. Knowing your unhelpful thinking style is important as the quicker you realize you are falling into your old trap, the quicker you can get out of it.

How to Rethink

The endless mind chatter is so very easy to get caught up in. I have already discussed that negative thoughts are here to stay so we know that the plan is not to try to eliminate those thoughts. The plan instead is to recognize when those thoughts arrive and then to lose our attachment to them.

The theory behind Acceptance and Commitment Therapy, or ACT, calls the art of detaching yourself from your thoughts as defusion. ACT is a psychological therapy that aims to maximize your potential for a rich, full and meaningful life. Part of the ACT approach is to redevelop your relationships with your thoughts by defusing from them. Defusion simply means to distance yourself or letting go from unhelpful thoughts.

The first step is to recognize the unhelpful thoughts. Unhelpful thoughts are basically thoughts that regardless if they are true or not, aren't helping you to maximize your life in according to your Why. A classic example is someone thinking they are overweight. It may be true for this particular person, but fixating on this thought is proving to be unhelpful. Instead, the person is dwelling on the situation, growing increasingly upset and frustrated, instead of taking inspired action. This person would be better to recognize that it is an unhelpful thought and focus on the positives, which may be making the appropriate life changes or focusing on their successes.

The second step is to recognize that they are just thoughts, and not the truth. We tend to take message in our head as the gospel truth. We get stuck in the story so much that we simply cannot see them for what they really are – thoughts. Sometimes our unhelpful thoughts are indeed true.

I've listed some strategies below to help you get started. Try them all and find which one works best for you. Each strategy will help you separate your holding onto your thoughts. They aren't the 'be all end all' but they are a very important step into changing our thought patterns. They will simply allow you to look at your thoughts differently and some may even make you laugh (which is a good thing!). These have been adapted from Russ Harris, 'ACT Made Simple.'

– **Thank your mind**. When you have an unhelpful thought, thank your mind for the thought. For example, "Thanks mind, I don't like that thought, I'm going to let that one go!"

– **Name the story**. If you notice you tend to have a lot of unhelpful thoughts around a particular topic or belief, give that story a name. For example, if you constantly berate yourself for not being beautiful enough, you might label that story 'the ugly story.' When the thoughts come again you can acknowledge that your mind is playing that story again – "Oh there's the ugly story again!"

– **Sing along**. Start singing the unhelpful thoughts to a funny tune.

– **Your bully**. Visualize your negative thoughts being said to you by a bully. Recognize that you are letting your thoughts, beliefs or ideas push you around, running your life and telling you what to do all the time. Would you let a bully do that to you?

– **Workability.** Does your thought work for you in pursuing your Why? Will it allow you to live a rich and meaningful life? Analyze the thought in relation to your Why.

– **What else are you getting?** When a thought shows up, and you go along with it, what feelings, thoughts or situations might it help you avoid or escape from in the long run?

– **Notice**. Notice what your mind is telling you right now and take a step back and look at this thought from the outside in.

– **iThought**. Imagine the thought is playing out on your computer, tablet or smartphone screen. Change the font, color and format, make the letters jump about, add emoticons.

– **Pew pew pew!** Visualize your troubling thought on a piece of paper, that has been pinned to a target. Visualize shooting that piece of paper with an arrow or gun until it is riddled with holes. Add sound effects. Guaranteed to make you laugh!

Should All Thoughts Be Let Go?

The idea of defusion is to lessen the impact of unhelpful thoughts. But the question remains: should we become attached to helpful thoughts or not?

We all tend to have a belief system that we hold close. Sometimes they are factual and other times, they are simply statements that we believe to be true, regardless if there are facts supporting them or not. We should all strive to be able to lessen the impact of all our thoughts on our decisions and in our life. Why? Because it invites us to be open minded and present in the moment.

Ultimately, it comes back to your Why. If your thoughts allow you to take inspired action towards your purpose, then they are helpful. Bear in mind though, that we are constantly evolving and learning as we go along. Something that we believe to be true, may prove later to be false. If you are too attached to that thought or notion, you will find it difficult to accept the new evidence. This can be stressful itself, giving you another unnecessary stressor to add to your list. Therefore, it's extremely helpful to recognize that all thoughts are just that – thoughts, not the unrelenting truth.

Real Women, Real Stories

Claire Yates, of Indinature

I am a nutritionist, author, recipe developer, speaker and soon to be commercial kombucha brewer. I think you can see by my varied job description I have a lot of things on!

The major stressors in my life can include:

- Lack of hours in the day to achieve what I need to get done. I seem to spend most weeks working 6 or 7 days.

– Feelings of anxiety and low self-esteem. I have always struggled with low self-esteem which is hidden by a very good front! This causes me a lot of stress and especially being more in the public eye…I am always questioning if I am good enough to be doing what I am doing.

– Financial pressure of running a small business and setting up the new kombucha (a fermented tea drink) business. We have got many dollars leaving us at the moment and not many coming back in yet!

– Meeting writing and media commitments/deadlines. I am currently finishing off an online program and also dealing with media commitments for the UK. This means lots of long hours and dealing with the UK time difference makes life very interesting!

I cope with my stressors through holistic means. I ALWAYS make getting a good night sleep my number one priority. Even when I have deadlines to meet, I know I work much better getting to bed by 9pm and up at 5am, rather than trying to pull an all-nighter. I also try to keep regular sleep hours both on weekdays and on weekends. Sleep really is my saviour!

Eating a well-balanced diet and getting essential nutrients to support my adrenals and serotonin production is also important. I make it a healthy habit to get outside to the local park with my husband and fuzzy kids (dogs). We walk the girls, get our feet in the grass and chat about our day, our business and anything else we need to talk about. This is great for calming my racing mind and easing my anxiety.

I also prioritise my workload and my deadlines. I use my smart phone and set reminders in my calendar for everything I have got coming up from client bookings, orders that need doing and bills that need to be paid. That way I don't have to stress about remembering, my phone does all the hard work!

Your Rethinking Checklist

– **Become aware of your thinking patterns.** Awareness is the first step to everything. Knowing how you think is vital as it allows you to recognize when you are getting caught in the story. Note down the events or situations that tend to trigger your negative thinking patterns.

– Try a defusion strategy. Try each of the defusion strategies listed above and note down which works best for you. Practice these daily until it becomes second nature to you.

– Practice mindfulness. As I've mentioned in the first chapter, mindfulness helps to get us out of our heads and into the moment. This is a great strategy to use when you're feeling stressed about the future.

– Keep a journal. Pour out your thoughts into a journal. It helps to 'empty the mind' and give you clarity of the thoughts going through your head. Hate writing? Record it on your phone. Going over these at a later date helps you to recognize irrational or unhelpful thinking.

– Write your stories. Using the 'Name The Story' technique, write out your stories for each persistent troubling thought you have. Write it in third person and give the story a happy ending. This will help you to look at the story from an outside perspective, allowing you to lessen its impact on you and your life.

– Share your thoughts with others. By sharing, you will realize just how normal your thoughts and worries really are. It will help you to realize that you are not alone and that together, we can all help each other cope better.

Chapter 7: Reaccept

"The best and most beautiful things in the world

cannot be seen or even touched.

They must be felt with the heart." – *Helen Keller*

Feelings are very powerful. Probably more powerful than thoughts. They consume our bodies and mind and can quite literally, paralyse us on the spot. Busy women are pretty good at either bottling all their emotions up inside, or being consumed by them. We can either be stone cold and heartless – or we are overly emotional, crying and despairing at the slightest inconvenience.

Whatever way we go, our handling of our emotions can be detrimental to our lives. Our stress levels are tightly associated with our emotions so it is important to learn how to manage our emotions effectively.

Accepting our feelings is all about allowing ourselves to have painful private experiences if and when doing so enables us to act on our Why. It always comes back to our Why.

The Problem With Avoiding

Being busy gives us a great excuse to avoid any type of feeling. We can turn into warriors with a mission when we do everything we can but to feel the pain that's brewing inside. We almost turn into robots. This is great in the short term but not so much in the longer term.

It's not just the bad feelings that are being avoided either. Many avoid feeling pure happiness or joy for a number of reasons: don't want to feel good because they feel that they don't deserve it, or worried that feeling too good will result in feeling really, really bad later because whatever goes up has to come down, right? Being fearful of our own feelings is a lot more common than we think.

The main issue with avoiding our emotions is that it's a fruitless exercise. We're never going to be able to eliminate negative feelings, just as we'll never eliminate negative thoughts. We instead need to focus on how we can manage our feelings in the most productive and healthiest way possible.

Do you have goals that sound like this:

> – I want to stop getting so angry all the time.

> – I just want to be happy.

> – I want to stop worrying.

> – I don't want to be anxious.

> – I want to be stress free.

These are 'emotional goals,' according to Russ Harris, a prolific researcher and Acceptance and Commitment Therapist. And they're very much the kind of goals you don't want to be striving for. Why? Because they focus on eliminating the negative emotion for good, and as I've explained already, that's completely fruitless. Our goals should be focused on learning how to respond or handle these emotions better.

Your Molotov Cocktail

Burning out is an impending reality for the stressed women who remain stressed. No one can last a long time by bottling their emotions up inside. You are in fact creating your own Molotov cocktail.

Imagine a real Molotov cocktail. A bottle is filled with flammable liquid, topped with a fuel-soaked rag, set alight and thrown at a vehicle or fortification. The bottle breaks, spraying fuel into the air and a fireball is produced, wreaking havoc wherever it lands.

Your bottled up feelings that are leading to a burn out are very much like throwing a Molotov cocktail. Your feelings are the flammable liquid inside the bottle. The rag represents the emotions that easily get you fired up – the ones that you find hard to contain, such as anger or frustration.

A stressful event occurs, maybe a relationship breakdown or an incident at work, that sets your anger or frustration alight. You feel thrown against the wall of life – and your bottle breaks. Your anger spreads like wildfire, lighting up all the emotions that are now pouring out of you. You have literally combusted into a breakdown. This is what happens when we bury our emotions deep inside. It's a bomb waiting to explode.

Accepting the Feeling

Learning how to embrace the full spectrum of feelings is, believe it or not, a hugely effective strategy to coping with stress. It is not about gritting your teeth and baring with the painful feelings. And it's not about liking the feeling. It's about letting your feelings travel their course. The more we fight our feelings, the more wasted energy we expend. Making peace with your feelings will allow you to make peace with your life.

When to Accept

It's a delicate situation when recognising when and how to accept our emotions. Ultimately, the idea isn't to passively accept our life situation.

It's not about accepting a feeling of sadness and despair and letting your life continue as it is. It's about acknowledging these feelings and then acting according to your Why to improve your life.

If the main stressors in your life are centered around a specific person, time or event, it is vital to know what feelings arise while learning how to make room for them.

If those feelings generally encourage you to take up negative, self-sabotaging behaviors such as binge drinking, overeating, worrying or ruminating, then learning how to breathe into your feelings and use your values to guide your choices will improve your stress response, and ultimately your life.

You may need to decide to either remove the challenging person, time or event from your life (if possible), or work on improving your relationship with the person, time or event.

Remember this: pursuing your Why is, without a doubt, going to produce circumstances that may prove painful for you. Life is all about balance – no matter how determined you are to have a 100% happy life, you will encounter challenges and tough times. Accepting this fact goes hand in hand with accepting the full spectrum of emotions in life.

Anxiety is one of the most difficult emotions to accept. Change almost always evokes anxiety so if we want to make changes in our lives, we need to accept the anxiety that comes with it. We cannot make the changes we desire if we are not willing to feel through that anxiety. One of my favourite quotes reminds me every day to embrace this feeling:

"Feel the fear, and do it anyway."

The strategies listed below can help you get started on developing a strong skill in accepting the feelings. They have been adapted from Russ Harris, the author of The Happiness Trap, a must-read book for all busy women.

– **Normalizing**. Remind yourself that it's perfectly normal to feel those feelings, and it shows that you are a normal human being who cares. Recognize that it's a feeling that happens when we don't get what we want.

– **Be compassionate with the feeling**. Treat it like a little puppy or crying child and hold it gently. Console it and let it pour.

– **The ladder**. Imagine you have a ladder with rungs. The higher the rung, the bigger the struggle. How much are you struggling with the feeling? How can you come down a few rungs to feel better?

– **Make room**. Make room for the feeling and allow it to sit there. Soften into it and let it flow. You don't necessarily have to like this but just let it flow through your body.

– **Helping hand.** Visualize your feeling as a glowing ball of electricity. Cup it into your hands and protect it, giving it a safe space to be until it's ready to go quiet.

– **Having a choice**. Consider having a choice to feel absolutely everything (both good and bad) or feeling nothing at all. Which would you rather?

– **Play with your feelings**. Be curious about your feelings. Find out where it is in your body, zoom in on it, where does it start and stop? Does it move around your body? Observe the feeling like it's not within your own body.

Real Women, Real Stories

Martyna Angell, of 'The Wholesome Cook'

Most people think that working as a recipe developer, tester and food photographer would mean that I get to feast on decadent foods each and every day. To an extent that's true, but it also more often than not means that I am working toward tight deadlines – stressing, cooking and shooting 6-8 recipes a day, with very little time left in the day for me to take the time out to breathe and actually eat.

So, to manage this, I began to schedule an actual 40-minute lunch break around the middle of my day when I would just walk across the road to the park or sit outside, away from my work area - the kitchen, and enjoy my meal with a recommended daily dose of vitamin D and a short walk to stretch and breathe whenever possible.

I realised that doing this was a great way to clear and re-energise my mind. My routine now also involved cooking up a batch of quick to grab veggies on the Sunday to have on hand during the busy weeks cooking and shooting. I also keep a few cans of tuna in pure olive oil and various raw salad greens on hand.

And, at the end of a stressful week like this I often like to switch off with a massage. Nourishing my sore muscles and enjoying a little me-time.

Your Reaccepting Checklist

This is a tough area to work on but like all others, it's very important. Our feelings are innately us – we will forever have them. The more you practice allowing and accepting the full range of feelings you experience, the better and more enriched your life will become.

– **Practice accepting strategies**. Much like the defusion list, try each strategy and find which ones work best for you. Then practice, practice, practice.

– **Find a safe space.** It can be quite confronting embracing strong feelings, particularly if you've been an avid avoider, so create or find a safe space where you can feel in private. Tears may flow, random spontaneous laughter may ensue so go somewhere private where you don't have to worry about other people judging you (you shouldn't anyway!).

– **Keep a journal.** Just as we discussed in your Rethinking checklist, journal your feelings regularly and consistently. Describe your emotions in terms of physical symptoms (shakes, tears, heart rate, shivers etc), impulses you may feel, related thoughts and whatever else happens. Be honest, be raw.

– **Learn to share.** Busy women can have a tendency to keep it all to themselves. It's isolating and not so good for keeping our stress levels short and sweet. Share your feelings with your closest friend or loved one. This is much like the idea of vulnerability, as explored in Brene Brown's research. The idea is to be open to your raw experiences and to share them with others. You will be pleasantly surprised at who opens up to you and holds you in their warm embrace.

– **Identify the feelings that arise during stressful times**. It can be helpful to recognize your natural emotional response to stressful situations, or the emotions you tend to experience prior to a stressful moment. Maybe it's fear of the unknown? Or joy that leads to feeling guilty for feeling happy because you've worked up a belief that you don't deserve to feel like that. Take note of these feelings and spend some time exploring these further.

Chapter 8: Reconnect

"I don't need anyone to rectify my existence.

The most profound relationship we will ever have

is the one with ourselves." - Shirley Maclaine

We're naturally social creatures. We always have been and we always will be. So it's no surprise that isolation and loneliness go hand in hand with chronic stress and unhappiness. Relationships come in a range of different forms and levels – friendships, lovers, family, acquaintances, colleagues. They all have a place in managing our stress.

Women in particular rely heavily on relationships (of all levels) for a myriad of reasons. But women are notorious for being extreme in their relationships, particularly with each other.

This isn't true for everyone but many busy, working women are prone to being very specific about who they regard as friends. Bitchiness, back-stabbing and competition rates high between women, and it's notorious in the corporate world.

It's a sad thing because not only does it create extra stress, it creates isolation and breeds resentment. It does nothing but create unhappiness. We are going to create a happier, healthier, more productive world for ourselves if we treat each other with the respect we all deserve.

The Beauty of Relationships

Relationships are all about connecting with other people. This can be through touch, communicating, sharing experiences or simply having an understanding between two people. It's a natural human response to desire connection with others and it is in fact an evolutionary trait that helped us get here today.

We do so much more much more effectively when we are connected to others. It does wonders for our health, lives and is essential in managing our stress.

There is physical evidence of how healing and beautiful stress-busting connecting with others really is. The hormone, oxytocin, which is also known as the 'cuddle hormone' is released when we hug someone. Kelly McGonigal explains in her TED talk that it makes you crave connections with loved ones, enhances your empathy and makes you compassionate and caring. It mimics emotions such as joy. What many people don't realize is that this hormone is actually a stress hormone.

Oxytocin is released when we are stressed. Your very own natural, inbuilt survival mechanism is actually encouraging you to seek support from others. It encourages you to notices when others are stressed so that you help each other out. Isn't that innately beautiful?

But get this – your heart has receptors for this hormone. Every time you reach out to someone to seek support or to help them, you release more and more of this hormone. The heart uses this hormone to regenerate and heal from any stress-induced damage.

Your amazing healing body has built its very own stress resilience mechanism to recover when its very own stress response is activated. We do not recognize nor appreciate the body's amazing ability to balance everything.

The take away is this: human connection is your key ingredient to recovery. Relationships not only provide us with meaning and experiences, they actually help us to heal.

Of course, it is important to have relationships that give you rich and meaningful experiences. Keep the ones who hold you high close, and the ones that drag you down, far.

When a Relationship Does More Harm than Good

Not all relationships are life enriching. In fact, they can completely drain our lives. We have all had those experiences where we feel obligated to begin, or continue, a relationship despite those relationships no longer serving us. They can be anything from family relationships to childhood friends to our work colleagues.

Knowing the good relationships from the bad is important. For every relationship in your life, you should be asking yourself these questions:

– Does this relationship serve me and my Why?

– Does this relationship help me to grow or does it hold me back?

– Does this relationship enrich my life and provide meaning?

– Does this relationship cause me unnecessary stress?

Keep in mind that no relationships are perfect. There will always be challenges in our relationships. The key is to identify the ones that are proving to be more challenging than rewarding. When you have identified your stressful relationships, it's then entirely up to you if you decide to end that relationship or attempt to mend that relationship. Do not feel that you have to mend every single relationship you have. It's completely alright to end relationships that no longer serve you.

Some relationships may feel like an obligation to you. This isn't necessarily a bad thing but it could be a challenge, depending on the status of that relationship. Family and work colleague relationships are classic examples. Family relationships, in particular, can be highly stressful. Whilst we may generally love our family members, sometimes we want to slap them silly! But as they say, family is blood and not exactly a relationship that we can choose. However, we can always choose how we approach that relationship.

If you find a family relationship is very stressful, you need to discover what it is exactly that is causing you so much stress.

– Is it their personality you can't stand?

– Are there unresolved issues?

– Do they have control over you?

Whatever it is will determine your next course of action. Leaving your relationships exactly the way they are will not change anything. You need to take steps to improve that relationship, particularly if it is important to you.

Of course, we cannot change the other person's opinions, responses or beliefs. We can only change our responses and work on our end of the relationship. I always recommend that if you take steps to improve your relationship with your family, and it does not resolve the way you would like, the next step is to then minimize the impact of that relationship on your life. It may be that you reduce your contact with that person or applying the Re-Approach to stress strategies to manage your stress response effectively. The strategies from the Rethinking and Reaccepting chapters will be highly valuable in these circumstances.

Self-Love

The most important relationship of all is the relationship you have with yourself. Busy women are brilliant at being their own worst enemy. We downplay our talents, highlight our weaknesses and constantly compare ourselves to others. We constantly belittle our own opinion and are quick to validate others criticisms of us. We are, quite literally, our biggest bully. Busy women are always, always striving for perfection.

The concept of self-love is learning how to develop and sustain a loving relationship with who we are. It's about acknowledging and accepting the imperfect beings we are. When we are filled with self-hate, we tend to treat ourselves (and those around us) with contempt. We simply cannot forge a positive attitude in life if we can't be positive towards ourselves.

Prolonged stress almost always has its roots in the poor relationship we have with ourselves. We are more likely to have less confidence, experience more negativity, harbor resentment and feel less secure when we are low on self-love.

The Curse of Comparisonitis

Self-hate can lead to a very dangerous, life threatening disease called 'Comparisonitis.' Ok, it's not going to kill you, but it sure isn't going to help you thrive. Comparisonitis is the art of comparing yourself to others who you perceive to be more successful, beautiful or simply better than you. Its symptoms include:

– The tendency to highlight every desired trait in your rival, of which you don't have;

– Stalking their social media outlets until you feel the depths of despair;

– Rating your self-worth in direct opposite to their success; and

– Rapidly declining confidence in your ability to reach the standard you are striving for.

It's a dangerous, dangerous disease. Why? Because it cripples you to the point of inertia.

Women are very, very good at comparing themselves to others. Society, in fact, encourages it. We are constantly bombarded with distorted messages from the 'Bigs' – Big Beauty, Big Fashion, Big Cosmetic, Big Food, Big Pharma.

The Bigs tell us that we should be supermodel thin, with flawless skin, picture perfect hair, with rock-hard abs. They also tell us we should have a full time career with a full time motherhood, and if we're a little too tired from that, pop this pill and be on your merry way.

The Bigs will do everything in their power to make us feel like we need to be a little more perfect.

This drive for perfection fuels the dreaded Comparisonitis. We constantly belittle our own beautiful uniqueness and strive to be a mass produced wonder woman who masters all. It's a recipe for failure. The rise of social media is compounding the effect. Do you spend time scrolling through your Instagram or Facebook feeds comparing yourself to those beautiful successful women touting their latest trip to paradise, or high end purchase? We seem to forget that we aren't looking at a realistic description of their lives. We are in fact looking at their highlight reel.

Busy women can particularly suffer from Comparisonitis in the workplace. It's the root of all that in house bitching I mentioned earlier in the chapter. Particularly for those in male-dominated industries, women are likely to become competitive with other women. This I believe, from talking to many women in the industry, has its roots in lack of self-love and a case of unrelenting Comparisonitis.

We scorn and bitch about our sisters because we feel threatened by them. We feel that they are going to get the promotion we are after or the recognition that we feel that we deserve. So instead of focusing on our work and improving our own performance, we find ways to bring their performance down to our level.

I genuinely believe that no woman wants to be like that. It's driven by our lack of self-love and not recognizing, or accepting, our own worth. When you learn to recognize your own value, you start to focus on growing. You no longer have time to bring others down because you are intent on being the best version of yourself.

The Social Game

Busy women have extraordinary social calendars. Work parties, children's games, coffee dates, weddings, engagements, baby showers, hens nights and the list goes on and on. We babes feel like we need to accept every invite we receive. This in itself can send our stress levels off the planet.

There are definitely benefits to being social, as I've already discussed, but the key is to know your limits. Some women thrive off a heavy, party-filled calendar. Others may see that same calendar and have a nervous breakdown. We are all different and we all have our preferences. Knowing your limits and being ok with these will help you find the balance in the social game.

Alone Time is OK

Isolation in general is pretty disastrous for our health and stress coping mechanisms. But the occasional down time alone can be really beneficial.

Being alone allows us a chance to reflect and be ourselves without judgment. When you do your time use diary, take note of the moments you have alone.

– Do you use these times to recharge?

– To reflect?

– To simply be?

The quietness of being alone can help restore our stress recovery. But be warned – alone time can stir up the negative self-hate if you give it the chance. Develop a mindfulness practice every chance you have an alone time.

Real Women, Real Stories

Alice Nicholls, of The Whole Daily

Stress management for me? It's probably best if I tell you how I used to manage stress. This will help to add colour to the whole 'stressful' situation.

I was stressed to the max about everything. I didn't know what I wanted to be when I grew up, I had dropped out of one university degree and was on the way to failing a second, I could never find a car park where i needed one, everyone had more than me, was prettier than I was and drove a better car.

I couldn't find my other shoe, the lift was broken, and traffic lights were always red, the last seat always taken. Stressed about everything.

So how did I manage this? I drank myself into oblivion each night, and smoke a packet of cigarettes each week while I was out in clubs that didn't shut until 9am.

I cried. A lot.

I nearly imploded. I was stressing my body physically by being unkind to it which meant I was stressed emotionally and lacked the health to function calmly when it came to anything, and beat myself up about anything and everything on a daily basis. A vicious cycle.

The biggest change for me was self-love and mindset. Firstly I made the conscious decision to make conscious decisions. I developed a gratitude practice for what I did have. I allowed myself to practice the concept that the universe will have its way. And I also started a practice in self-love.

No car park? Perfect, I must need to walk a bit more today. Life broken? Good, it may have been a death trap. Would love want me to drink until I couldn't speak? No way. "I love myself unconditionally in this moment."

The bottom line for me is that I have control over something and can change it. If I do not have control over something and I can't change it, I don't stress about it because I love myself too much to carry the stress.

In fact, it all comes back to self-love. The practice itself needs to be made anew. So when I find myself tested by situations that may invoke stress, I take a deep breath and work this this practice in mind.

Your Reconnecting Checklist

Managing your relationships is very important to managing your stress. They can either help or hinder our lives. These strategies can be implemented alongside Reaccepting and Rethinking strategies, as you will find that relationships generally tend to stir up our emotions and beliefs.

– **Keep those close that hold you high.** Know who are the most important people in your life and consciously acknowledge their existence. Thank them and be grateful for them every day. Invite these people into your life, and selectively choose who you want to be vulnerable with. Never ever go alone in life. Stress loves isolation and will breed and grow stronger every time you choose to go alone.

 – **Distance yourself from those that drag you down**. There are people that just don't get it. You can't change them, nor should you try. The best thing for you to do is to distance yourself from them as much as possible. Can't because they're family or the boss? Minimise your interactions with them as much as possible.

 – **Know your social limits.** It's completely ok to not be the social butterfly. Plan your social calendar with a priority list. Attend those that you feel are the most important, or better, the most enjoyable for you to attend. Politely decline all events that are low on your priority list. Know that it's completely ok to decline an offer if you'd rather sit in your bathtub at home.

 – **Develop a daily gratitude practice for your relationships.** Even the most meaningful, enriching relationships can give us challenging times. Remind yourself daily of the beauty those relationships bring you. You will notice your relationships are further enriched from this simple act, and you will eliminate unnecessary stress through appreciating the beauty of your relationships. Even when they're annoying you to bits!

 – **Build your self-love muscle.** Pump it every day babe, every single day. Create a self-love daily affirmation that is meaningful to you. For example, 'I am beautiful inside and out' or 'I am worthy of this career.' Put it on a post-it note or write it on your mirror and say it to yourself every single day. Keep saying it until you believe it.

– **Beware of comparisonitis.** It's a pretty evil disease. Don't let it grab a hold of you because it does nothing but fuel your stress. Keep it in check, particularly at work.

– **Be kind.** Trust me, it goes a long way. You never know what great relationship you may invite into your life if you are simply kind to someone. Wouldn't you rather be remembered as the kind lady instead of 'that bitch' anyway?

– **Become aware of your behaviors in relationships**. We tend to notice in others what we seek in or believe we have in ourselves. For example, if you strive to be the next CEO of your company, you will notice all the traits you believe to be important in order to get that promotion (such as leadership or assertiveness skills) in your colleagues. This may provoke Comparisonitis behaviors and could quite literally destroy a positive relationship you may have with a colleague. Be wary of this and recognize when it is your actions that are causing strain on your relationships.

Chapter 9: Replenish

Nature is a wonderful thing. The vast beauty of nature in the world is breathtaking. Watch any nature documentary and your mind is blown with the diversity of this planet. We, as human beings, are part of this natural landscape. Whilst we may like to think we are superior and that this is 'our world,' we are in fact just another element in this natural world.

Replenishing ourselves in nature is important in maximizing our health and stress responses. We generally tend to live in large built-up environments, anything from bustling big cities to regional towns. Buildings may go as far as the eye can see with only a splattering of natural landscapes.

The lucky ones, in my eyes, are the ones that have a wealth of nature on their doorstops. Those who live near the coast, on a farm, in small towns or even next to a large park. The not-so-lucky ones are the ones living in high rises or apartment blocks. Because to get your healthy dose of nature, you need to actively seek it out. And if you want to be healthy, stress better and have a more rewarding life, then you need to get back in touch with nature.

Biophilia

Nature, in its essence, is a community of living organisms. We, as human beings, have a relationship with everything in nature. In fact, we actively seek it. According to Edward O. Wilson, an American biologist and researcher, the term 'biophilia hypothesis' proposes that there is an instinctive bond between human beings and other living systems. This includes plants, animals, weather and the solar system.

Biophilia explains why we have a natural tendency to prefer natural things. For example, we go all gooey-eyed over baby animals. Their big wide eyes and small features instantly make us want to pick them up and cuddle them until they grow older. All adults mammals (we are mammals, remember?) do this across species.

It's an evolutionary thing – we'd probably kill a species to extinction if all those baby animals looked more delicious than cute (sorry vegans, but it's true). Biophilia also explains why we sometimes risk our lives to save other animals lives, or keep plants and flowers in the home. Our natural love for life, in all its forms, helps to sustain it.

But why is this relevant to stress, productivity and general awesomeness of life? The whole Re-Approach is about going with our natural stress mechanisms, instead of working against it. Having a relationship with nature is going with our very own nature. We naturally seek to heal, therefore it makes sense that our environment, which we intuitively seek, is going to help us heal from stress and bad habits.

Numerous studies show the benefits of nature to our health. A study from the University of Rochester published in Personality and Social Psychology argues that paying attention to the natural world makes people feel better and also makes them behave better. Research shows that taking a stroll through a natural setting can boost performance on activities requiring sustained focus.

Another study by University of Michigan researchers demonstrated that, after just an hour interacting with nature, memory performance and attention spans improved by 20 percent. Researchers at the University of Kansas reported a 50 per cent boost in creativity for people who were steeped in nature for a few days. Nature, quite simply, has hidden benefits that we do not consciously appreciate.

The Healing Power of Animals

Oh, animals, you gotta love them. You do not truly appreciate how loving, rewarding and enriching a pet can be until you own one. They have their own unique personalities and very quickly become a member of your family. And they are excellent for helping us to stress better.

Research shows that, unless you're someone who really dislikes animals or is absolutely too busy to care for one properly, pets can provide excellent social support, stress relief and other health benefits. Having a pet improves your mood (those big puppy eyes can make anyone melt with love), starves off feeling of loneliness and encourages you to get outside and move.

Dogs in particular are great as exercise buddies. I have a two year old kelpie that needs a run every single day. No matter how tired or lazy I'm feeling, she needs that run and consequently, I end up taking her for a walk. A walk that I wouldn't have done if I didn't have her big puppy dog eyes sucking me in (or a backyard littered with holes).

Having a pet obviously doesn't work for everyone. In fact you may find having a pet more stressful than rewarding! If you are someone that genuinely likes animals and cannot have a pet for whatever reason, don't feel like you cannot experience the benefits of connecting with animals.

There are other ways to experience the joy of animals – go to your local park and feed the ducks, or sit outside and listen to the birds. Maybe you could set up a bird bath in your backyard. Or visit a local animal shelter or animal farm with the kids. Interaction with other animals will help you to manage your stress better so aim to include it regularly in your life.

The Sun Vitamin

The sun is a wonderful thing. It is the elixir of life that feeds the Earth. It is also vital to our health. The sun is the biggest natural source for our vitamin D stores. Vitamin D, which is actually a hormone and not a vitamin, is beneficial to our bodies in a myriad of ways. It helps our immune system, strengthens our bones, regulates the absorption of calcium and phosphorus in our bodies and aids in cell to cell communication. It's also essential in maintaining a healthy body weight and plays a key part in helping our brain work well.

Essentially, vitamin D is required to be healthy in body and mind, therefore imperative in our stress management.

Vitamin D deficiency leads to conditions such as osteoporosis, heart disease and certain types of cancer. And it's a lot more common than we think. Elderly people and those with dark skin produce less vitamin D. Those who live in the Northern Hemisphere may struggle to produce enough vitamin D in the winter.

The good news is that you can supplement vitamin D if you cannot get enough sun exposure. However, you should try to get direct sun exposure when you can. The natural source is always better and more effective than any man-made source. Of course, this needs to be just enough to get your vitamin D hit without getting burnt! Go outside for 20 minutes on a sunny morning without any sun protection.

Office Woes

So you're a busy woman. I imagine you spend a significant portion of your time indoors, whether it's in an office, in the home or elsewhere. I also imagine that you spend a significant portion of your time with technology. You may have a smart phone, a tablet, laptop, a music player, radios, computers, TVs and whatever else comes out on the market tomorrow. Essentially, I'm sure you spend a lot more time in a man-made environment than the natural environment.

As I have covered in this chapter so far, the natural environment has a lot of healing wonders for our bodies and minds. The man-made, technical environment doesn't appear to have this same kind of healing mechanism. There is a growing body of evidence that technology, in particularly electromagnetic radiation (EMF), can be harmful to our health. Mobile phones and wireless technologies are common technologies that transmit dangerous levels of EMF. In general, high artificial EMFs have been shown to disturb the human body's natural energetic field, leading to stress and fatigue as well as DNA changes and degenerative diseases like cancer. Studies have also shown that EMF exposure can lead to weakened immune systems. This is not so good for our ability to manage stress effectively.

The only way to reduce the harmful effects of EMF is to limit your exposure. Going completely EMF-free is realistically not possible, unless you're willing to pack up the family home, move to the bush and live like a hermit off the land.

Make it a daily practice to have technology-free times throughout the day. Yes, that means leaving your phone behind for a bit. I'm aware that mobile phones are our new limbs but believe me – you can survive without it for a little while! I also implore you to never sleep with your phone next to your bed. It impairs your ability to sleep properly, and we know how important sleep is, don't we ladies?

Real Women, Real Stories

Anita Byrne, Employment Insight

So I'm pretty busy and didn't even realise how busy until reflection! I have, in the last 2 years, made 3 overseas and several interstate trips; moved house twice; started/ran 2 businesses... the list goes on! It was during this time that I learnt how to recognize stress and how to manage it.

In the past, stress has been the result of these busy, busy periods and has led to Glandular Fever (including GF's reoccurring symptoms), chronic hay fever, anxiety and digestion issues. Of course all of the above came into full force during the last 2 years - so I decided to learn more about my mind, body and spirit!

People used to ask me why I never looked stressed, with so many things going on, and I used to believe them and think that I wasn't. I've realised since, that I'm a closet stressor! I didn't even think I was stressed – then I walked into a Naturopaths office and she asked me why I wasn't breathing. (Of course I was breathing!?) But I wasn't. AND my shoulders were up around my ears!

As a Career Coach I work with a lot of younger clients starting out in their career after leaving school or Uni. They often don't know where to start! So initially I work with them on 'them.' One day I realised that I hadn't even worked on this myself and so came the journey of what's important to me. I discovered that above all; Health, Love + Creativity were the most important things to me, in my life. Well, being stressed could not possibly add value to my 'health,' maybe an outlet for my 'creativity' would help reduce my stress and if I truly do 'love' myself I will do anything to work on this. Ah-ha moment!

Working with job seeking clients, I discuss techniques to overcome stress. I adopt these in my own life, as well as other techniques - and the most important ones for me are:

– The self-actualization, being in the present and detoxifying elements of Yoga;

– The peace and clarity of mind that comes with Meditation

– Balance! Balance of life – Health/Exercise, Relationships, Work, Play, Meditation, Spirituality. Whatever your life involves.

I love being in nature and one of my favourite things to do is bushwalking. This soothes my soul and has allowed me to take photographs in tucked away places all over the world.

That is where my 2nd business came into manifestation. Not only that, there is something about allowing Mother Nature to take away all of your stress, negativity and worries and then replenishing you with her positive energy and strength.

Whenever I reflect on the balance of my life and notice I'm toppling over, the stress will often rear its ugly head - so I identify it, re-align by using any or all of the above and I carry on with happiness in the fact that I control my life - and stress doesn't.

The mantra I often adopt is; "Let it come, let it go, let it flow."

Your Replenishing Checklist

Getting your nature hit is going to be the easiest of all the Re-Approach areas. But it's also the easiest to not consciously acknowledge its value. Combine all your new stress management strategies with nature – go outside to exercise, meditate on a patch of grass, have a picnic in the park. Just remember to be grateful for the beautiful world you live in.

– Get outside. Pretty obvious but try to get outside as much as you can, every single day. Couple this with your re-energising tasks, like going for a walk in the park or riding to work.

– Go barefoot. If you're lucky enough to live near the beach, you'll find this easy. For those who don't have this glorious option, find a patch of grass and let your toes breathe.

– **Buy a grounding mat.** If going outside or going barefoot really isn't your thing, then you might like these. Grounding mats are mats that replicate the earth's energy vibrations, which are said to be beneficial for our health and reducing our stress levels. You can even use them under your desk so kick off your heels and get grounded whilst being a wonder woman!

– **Get some sun.** Working long hours from dusk to dawn means we aren't getting the Vitamin D we so desperately need.. Make it a habit to go outside to simply get some sunshine. If you live in a sunny, tropical haven, try to get some sunshine without any sunscreen on. But be sure to slip, slop, slap after 10-20 minutes to ensure you don't burn.

– **Get a pet.** Only if you can look after it of course. Pets are fabulous at reducing our stress levels and can bring immense happiness into our lives. Don't have the time for a pet but love animals? Make it a habit to get in contact with animals whenever you can, even if it means going to the local park to see dogs in their element.

– **Bring the outside in.** Potted plants make amazing décor. They not only look fabulous, but they clean and purify our air. Place pot plants indoors wherever you can and keep a bunch of fresh flowers on your desk. The smell, look and feel can be incredibly effective at reducing your stress.

– **Get dirty**. Create a garden in your backyard. You can do this regardless of how small it is – there are many books out there that can help you to create gardens in small spaces. Create an edible garden. Not only will you reap the benefits of reconnecting with nature, you will grow your own food. It's like growing money!

– Reduce your EMF exposure. Turn your phone and Wi-fi connections off at night. Use hands-free on your phone, use landlines when you can and have internet-free time. When you are outside and in nature, leave your phone behind. If that isn't practical, at least turn your phone onto airplane mode.

Kate's Final Message

"In three words, I can sum up everything I've learned about life:

it goes on" – Robert Frost

The key factor of this Re-Approach is to make small changes in all eight areas. I have given you plenty of strategies to try. Choose the ones that make the most sense to you, but don't forget this: you need to make positive changes in all eight areas to really see improvement.

You may prefer to focus on one area more than others, but do not completely neglect an area. Life is all about balance and so is your new stress management, healthy habit creating regime.

To make it a little easier for you, here is an outline of an action plan you can start implementing immediately.

1. Finish this book.

2. Schedule your VIP appointment.

3. Prepare for your VIP appointment by completing your Time Use diary over five-14 days.

4. Hold your VIP appointment.

5. Refocus on your Why and be reminded of it every day. This drives EVERYTHING.

6. Start implementing Re-Approach strategies immediately.

7. Ensure all eight areas are covered.

8. Create your healthy habits, one step at a time.

9. Check in with yourself regularly. Schedule your VIP appointment every three to six months.

10. Reward yourself daily.

I wish I could give you a detailed action plan. I simply cannot do that until I know your Why, your circumstances, preferences, ideals and well, you. This is as generic as I can be whilst being as helpful as I can be.

I sincerely hope this book helps you to improve your life. Stress isn't really a bad thing after all, when we use it right. Bad habits will start to give way to healthy habits when we stress better. I look forward to hearing your stories on how you re-approached your stress management, and ultimately your life, and started to see the results you have always wanted.

Remember that it takes time and commitment to get the changes you are searching for. This isn't a magic pill – they do not exist. I have faith that you have everything it takes to do whatever it is that you need to do. I sincerely hope this book has given you all the basic tools you need to see incredible changes in your life.

If you enjoyed this book and found that it has helped you to become the best version of yourself, please feel free to share your stories on my blog, www.summersaltlife.com.au/blog. Your story will inspire your fellow working women to take the leap they have been searching for.

We're all in this together. If you know a fellow woman who could do with a little extra support and advice in managing her busy life, you may want to let her know that this book is available on Amazon. If you enjoyed it, please leave a review if you could; it helps me to share this much-needed message to, what I like to call, the worldwide sisterhood. Because together, we can make an impact!

To your happiness,

Kate Toholka

Speaker, Author, Health Coach & Occupational Therapist.

Summersaltlife.com.au

About the Author

Kate Toholka

I was born in Castlemaine, Australia to hard-working parents. My mother, a veterinarian, and my father, an ex-Air Force man and business guru, brought me and my older brother, a doctor, up in a beautiful small town north of Melbourne. I credit my independence and drive to help others to my loving upbringing.

At 10 months of age, I became violently ill with bacterial meningitis. I was lucky to escape with my life. As a consequence, I lost a lot of my hearing. It proved challenging growing up, where I learnt how to handle bullies and indifferent looks at my hearing aids by learning to be strong. I believe this unique experience and the challenges my hearing loss has given me, has equipped me to have a greater understanding of how to manage stressful life events.

At the age of 18, I started my Occupational Therapy degree at university. I was completely out of my comfort zone. Large theatre rooms, new people, and an overwhelming party lifestyle. I partied hard. I broke hearts and got mine broken along the way. I became withdrawn, horrified at who I was becoming. I was incredibly self-conscious, avoiding having my hair up because I hated the looks I would get from people. I put on a lot of weight, I became depressed and highly anxious all the time. My stress levels were through the roof.

By the time I'd turned 21, I started to slow down. I subconsciously took note of all the negatives in my life and I gradually detoxed them for good. I left old so-called 'friendships' behind and made new, better friends. I met the love of my life and curbed my partying. I graduated from university, not with flying colours, but I still managed to score one of the best jobs available for a new graduate. I was now with my first full-time job in an area I loved (mental health), in a loving relationship and I was a lot happier.

I wasn't completely satisfied though. I longed to get out of the city. 18 months into my position we made the decision to move to the coast at the end of my two year contract. And it was the best decision I made. I fell in love with nature, got myself fit and created more loving relationships. I found a passion for holistic living and realised that this was the answer I was looking for.

2013 saw my spiritual awakening. For someone who is more scientific-minded than spiritual, this was big. I rediscovered my Why – my purpose is to help women be the best versions of themselves and to do it together. I completed my Holistic Health Coaching qualification, and met even more amazing souls. It was also the year I decided to start my own business. Stress was a constant and it was something I needed to work on. Utilising the strategies I have listed throughout this book, I reapproached my stress with success. Every day, I work with my stress, not against it. I now have all the tools I need to live my life exactly how I want.

I worked hard on finding my true self. I know how hard it can be and it really is a journey, not a destination. I love working closely with women –busy working women just like you – to achieve their goals. I get what I call my 'coaches high' after a session with my client. It's a buzz that makes me feel alive – a buzz that is reminding me that I'm living in according to my Why. I love nothing more than to see my sisters breaking free of their self-imposed restraints, letting their beauty shine in the world. You, my sister, have so much potential. If only you really knew it.

Connect with Kate

www.summersaltlife.com.au

www.facebook.com/summersaltlife

Instagram: www.instagram.com/summersaltlife

Twitter: www.twitter.com/summersaltlife

PS: Don't forget to visit the website to get all you free videos and extra free resources to help you Re-Approach.

www.summersaltlife.com.au/healthyhabits

Password: healthyhabits

Acknowledgements

Firstly I would like to acknowledge Pam and Steve Brossman for helping bring this book to life. There is no way I could have done this without their support. Thank you for teaching me how to not only write this book, but to get it into as many hands as possible. Thank you for welcoming me into your Best Sellers family!

Secondly, thanks to Timmy for having faith in me and my dreams. I couldn't do this without you. Hershey, our beloved kelpie pup, is forever my source of inspiration and happiness. We can learn so much from our beloved companions about health and living a low-stress life.

To my lifelong friends Jess, Beth, Alex, Georgia, Cassie, Cristina, Ash, Clare, Ash and Kathryn for believing in me and dealing with all my crazy life changes. Elise, can't wait to bring the Sisterhood movement with you to the world.

To all my Aussie classmates of January 2013 IIN intake. You've inspired me to take my life to the next level. Alice Nicholls, Lynn Gilmartin, Nicole Beardsley, Ali Clyne, Angie Lie and Kim MacPherson – you are the girls that keep me straight and focused. You are all game changers and together we will transform the world to a happier, healthier place.

It's a funny thing that I owe a depth of gratitude to a social media platform but Instagram has enabled so many opportunities for me. It's connected to me to so many beautiful souls. Belle Gibson, Natasha Mason, Sarah Jenkins, Tully

Humphries, Nicky Done, Jamie Gonzalez, Bianca Dye, Amy Crawford and the list goes on.

To the lovely ladies who have willingly contributed their own stories to this book: Suzzi Hartery, Sally-Anne Blanshard, Claire Yates, Shakti Grace, Alice Nicholls, Erin Smallbon, Anita Byrne, Martyna Angell and Elise Carver. Your honesty is going to help so many women.

Thanks to Oliver Freeman for managing to take a nice photo of me for my cover. You've got talent.

HEALTHY HABITS

ONLINE PROGRAM

ALIVE. ENERGISED. HEALTHY. HAPPY.
FIT. SLIM. PRODUCTIVE. IN LOVE.
INSPIRED. MOTIVATED. FREE.
VIBRANT. SUCCESSFUL.
INDEPENDENT. HEART-DRIVEN.
CONFIDENT. PROUD. BLISSFULLY
CONTENT.

Create your healthiest habits with this online 8 week support program. Includes workbooks, supportive forum, videos and a whole lot more.

Visit www.summersaltlife.com.au/shop for more information

and the next groups starting date.

SPECIAL OFFER

Receive a 15% discount to the next Healthy Habits 8 Week Program!

Email **kate@summersaltlife.com.au** with the code:

#HealthyHabitDiscount as your subject heading to receive this

offer.

(NB: Not available for VIP spots)

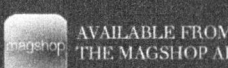 

NOTES

NOTES

Lightning Source UK Ltd.
Milton Keynes UK
UKOW06f0855150515

251609UK00012B/333/P